NO
SELF
NO
PROBLEM
WORKBOOK

NO
SELF
NO
PROBLEM
WORKBOOK

Exercises & Practices From Neuropsychology and Buddhism To Help You Lose Your Mind

CHRIS NIEBAUER, PhD

Hierophantpublishing

Cover design by Adrian Morgan
Cover art by Shutterstock
Print book interior design by Frame25 Productions

Ponzo illusion by Frame25 Productions
Shaded squares by Frame25 Productions

Hierophant Publishing
San Antonio, Texas
www.hierophantpublishing.com

If you are unable to order this book from your local bookseller, you may order directly from the publisher.

Library of Congress Control Number: 2022910060
ISBN: 978-1-950253-35-7

10 9 8 7 6 5 4 3 2 1

The ability to think about what is not happening is
a cognitive achievement that comes at an emotional cost.
—Matthew A. Killingsworth and Daniel T. Gilbert

Contents

Introduction

The Clouds of Thought

What's the strangest thing about being a conscious human being?

For me, it's that, to most people, it doesn't seem strange at all. When we consider what it means to be alive and conscious in a mysterious universe, we should be motivated to run through the streets yelling, "I'm a conscious being!" Yet we do no such thing. Remarkably, as we go about our day-to-day lives, consciousness seems normal, common, and in most instances the uniqueness of it goes unnoticed entirely.

Perhaps this is due to consciousness being cloud-hidden by the thinking mind. When I say the thinking mind, I mean the voice in your head, which spends most of its time interpreting the world it perceives, rather than actually experiencing it. While the thinking mind began as a useful tool in our evolutionary survival, it now acts as an obstacle, as nearly all of us live our lives confusing who we truly are with the interpreting voice in our heads. Furthermore, I believe that this misidentification causes virtually all the unhappiness, depression, and anxiety we ever experience.

It doesn't have to be like this, however.

According to the teachings in Buddhism, Taoism, and certain schools of Hindu philosophy, our true essence lies far beyond the limitations of the thinking mind. Recent findings in neuroscience have finally caught up to these ancient ideas.

My goal for this workbook is that it will serve as a tool to help you go beyond the veil of thought and reconnect you with the experience of what I like to call *clear consciousness*, or those moments when you are living entirely in the present moment, neither controlled by nor obsessed with the voice in your head.

As the title suggests, this is a companion to my previous book, *No Self, No Problem: How Neuropsychology Is Catching Up to Buddhism*, but don't worry if you haven't read it yet. You can begin with this one and the hands-on exercises and practices within it. Both books draw on the current understanding in neuroscience involving the left and right brain. The left side of the brain constantly interprets the world and tells stories to explain it. This way of thinking is sometimes called L-mode, the interpreting mind, or the thinking mind; and while both sides of the brain work together in some capacity all the time, for simplicity's sake I will often refer to this way of thinking as left-brained. The left brain tells stories, and then endeavors to solve the problems it believes arise out of the stories it has created. Most of the time, it uses language to create these stories.

But the most convincing (and overlooked) story the left brain tells is arguably the most important. It tells the story of you, or who you think you are. Remarkably, findings in neuroscience now suggest that the story we tell of ourselves, or what we think of as our self, is an illusion, albeit a *very* convincing one. As you will soon see, it is the thinking mind that creates the idea of a self along with most, if not all, of the problems we experience as humans.

While neuropsychology has only recently made this discovery of an illusory self, this concept was in fact the subject of a lecture given twenty-five hundred years ago by the Buddha on *anatta,* or "no self." Many consider this the most important teaching of Buddhism. This revelation is present in other Eastern philosophies as well, such as Hinduism, Taoism, and Jainism, and similar ideas can be found in the more esoteric traditions within Christianity, Judaism, and Islam. The famous thirteenth-century Sufi poet and mystic Rumi also alludes to losing one's sense of self:

> Although you appear in earthly form
> Your essence is pure Consciousness.
>
> . . .
>
> When you lose all sense of self
> the bonds of a thousand chains will vanish.[1]

All these traditions agree that when the self is revealed to be an illusion, it also shows how the problems the self created are illusions too. Put another way, much of our mental suffering is a fabrication, created and perpetuated by our thinking minds.

While some of the Buddha's students are said to have become immediately enlightened by his lecture on *anatta* (the doctrine of no self), most of us aren't so lucky. We have incorrectly linked our left-brained thinking mind with our sense of self for so long that we require a little more to undo this illusion and the problems it creates. In fact, learning about the idea of no self can become just another thought in the swirling chaos of thoughts in our minds.

This book aims to unpack and explore the thinking mind and move toward our ultimate goal, which is to integrate everything we are (brain, body, emotions, and more) and live in the mystery and wonder of clear consciousness.

Of course, in order to understand and go beyond the thinking mind, we cannot use the thinking mind—at least not solely. At the same time, we can't stop thinking, as much as we might like to. We can, however, open the door to a different kind of knowing, one that is far more experiential and grounded in the present moment.

This book offers an array of exercises and practices to help you do just that. The exercises will expose how the thinking mind operates, how it's often not as smart as it "thinks" it is, and how it creates problems in your life by thinking. The practices in this book, on the other hand, are designed to help you go beyond the mind. The word *practice* implies doings that are to be experienced rather than thought about, and also things that can't be done perfectly. The left brain chafes at these because it prefers perfection (and of course it has its own idea of what perfection is!). *Practice* also implies an ongoing aspect, which is essential; you will never be "finished." In addition, experiencing is much more important than thinking when it comes to practice. The left brain is going to tell you that these practices are silly. It will try to predict their outcomes and shut down the process of doing to protect itself and its illusions. That's okay; it's only doing what it was designed to do. But it's important to actually *do* these practices, even if they feel obvious. Buddhism has taught us the importance of direct experience when it comes to insight and change. We know this from sports too. You literally can't think your way to a better golf swing. You have to just do it. Simply thinking more about our thinking problems can't get us anywhere.

Speaking of thinking, for most people, thoughts take the form of language. That is, we experience them as a voice in our head, as if we are talking to ourselves. Language is fundamental to our lives—we talk to each other, and we use technologies as simple as the written word and as complex as videos on the internet to expand the reach of our language through time and space. Language is also a central tool in the creation of the fictitious self. The left side of the brain does most of this talking because it is the side of the brain that processes language. In doing so, the left brain often draws us away from our immediate physical reality by telling stories about anything and everything—but most of these stories are about the past or future. The left brain doesn't like the immediacy of the present.

We will explore the mind's use of language throughout this book, but for now I think it's safe to say that the left brain keeps the illusion of the self alive and well largely by way of its fascination with words (perhaps even its addiction to words). Perhaps we can use language as a tool to gain access to no self. To that aim, some of the practices in this book will consist of changing our language to more accurately describe our reality. While I am not suggesting that changing our language alone can fix the problem, I do think we can use language to expand our limited understanding of the self.

We know that the part of the brain that engages when we talk to others is the same part that activates when we talk to ourselves.[2] This is a small part of the left brain called Broca's area. The ongoing chatter of our thoughts might feel like a harmless, pesky fly. However, if we take our thoughts seriously, that chatter can become a never-ending source of anxiety, depression, and suffering. If, on the other hand, we learn to see our thoughts as impersonal electrochemical reactions that are happening in our brains (some of which are helpful and some of which are not), we can begin to free ourselves from the suffering they cause. Human evolution has greatly benefitted from our ability to ruminate on the past and anticipate the worst possible future. For eons, it was important to take each thought seriously, even if it made life difficult. Human survival looks different today than it did when our left brain evolved; perhaps the next step in our evolutionary journey is to change our relationship with our own thinking mind for the better. We won't shut the left-brained programming off, but we will learn to integrate it into the understanding of the right brain. By integrating the two, we return home to clear consciousness.

Lastly, I want to be clear that this book is not a typical book on cognitive science, an interdisciplinary field that brings together philosophy, neuroscience, and psychology. Cognitive science only came into being in the 1960s, and it focuses on the thinking mind and what it does, or *cognition.* As defined by psychologist Ulric Neisser, cognition is "those processes by which the sensory input is transformed, reduced, elaborated, stored, recovered, and used." Modern cognitive science knows explicitly that our thoughts are not perfect reflections of reality but rather transformed interpretations. It's a big leap for most humans to accept this, and I hope through using this book it will become easier. In any case, *please do not try to memorize anything in this book—that is not the point.*

I've also intentionally simplified the concept of left brain/ interpreting mind/thinking mind into something we can clearly see and work with to alleviate suffering and elevate our consciousness and well-being. In my own life, the convergence of neuroscience and Buddhist wisdom and practice has flowered into profound peace, understanding, joy, and ongoing curiosity. I consider this the greatest gift of my existence, and I hope to offer you some keys that might open similar doors in your own life.

Before we dive into this journey, I want to offer a simple practice: focusing on doing less. There is great power in small steps.

Practice: The Power of Small Moves

How often have you made a resolution to change something about your life, and committed to what feels like a realistic goal, only to find that it falls apart in weeks or months? Flossing your teeth, eating more healthy meals, keeping up with exercise, devoting time to a passion or creative project—want to do something? Do less.

Because the left brain likes to plan and worry, sometimes when you decide to do something to make a change, the mind will rev up into all kinds of self-destructive thoughts and stories: *I've never been able to keep the weight off. Mindfulness just doesn't work for me.* This is the left brain trying to control and protect you; it's not doing anything wrong. But there's a way to bypass the thinking mind so that you can make steady progress. Instead of setting a goal to meditate for an hour a day, decide to take just one conscious breath. Instead of sitting down with the intention of having a mindful meal, take one mindful bite. Instead of planning to floss every day, tell yourself you're going to floss one tooth. Seriously.

The left brain will consider any of these tiny actions to be "meaningless," and will often let go of the result. *Sure. One tooth. Knock yourself out.* And yet, once you have the floss out and get into that tooth, the body memory and whole brain may see that you might as well finish the job. Accomplishing a tiny step will cost you nothing, and often can get you over the hump of planning, anticipation, and negative self-talk that are the real enemies of forward progress. Just do the tiniest thing you can and see what happens.

As we begin, please approach things from the perspective that small moves can make a big difference.

Waking Up to Mind

What do you do when you meet a new friend? Perhaps you make a coffee date to get to know each other better, and you settle into a nice pair of comfy chairs near the back of the café. Where do you begin? With stories, of course. You might tell each other where you grew up, what your parents do for a living, or how you were raised. You might tell stories about your education or your career path, as well as more recent stories about your marriage, your children, etc. Your new friend may do the same. Even a short conversation along these lines can lead to a sense of closeness and understanding between people. These are the stories that we believe make us who we are. Each of us is telling the story of "me."

This "me" is the central figure in the stories we share at coffee shops, at work, and most importantly, in our own minds, over and over again. "Me" is a story created by the remarkable left brain. But like a sword that cuts both ways, the thinking mind's greatest accomplishment has also led to its biggest downfall, as virtually all of the mental suffering we ever experience can be traced back to this idea of "me."

This is where the Buddha and others have made a contribution to our species that is unmatched in the modern evolutionary period. They have shown us that this idea of me, produced by the thinking mind, is in fact an illusion, and that seeing through this illusion is the key to lessening, if not eliminating, our suffering.

This is a bold claim for sure, and one that I examine in detail in my previous book, *No Self, No Problem*. It's the basis for the exercises and practices in this book that aim to expose this illusion and help you experience clear consciousness as the no self.

But before we get started, let's review how neuropsychology inadvertently discovered the fictitious self.

If you call up an image of the human brain in your mind, you will likely see one of its key features, which is that the brain has two mirrored halves. These halves are connected by a set of 800 million nerve fibers called the corpus callosum. In the 1960s, a group of doctors and researchers aiming to mitigate the effects of severe epilepsy theorized that seizure activity crossed from one side of the brain to the other over the corpus callosum. Doctors Roger Sperry and Michael Gazzaniga believed that by cutting this bridge between the two sides of the brain, seizures would be easier to control. They were correct, and Sperry would win the Nobel Prize in 1981 for this work.

One result of these surgeries was that researchers now had access to a group of patients whose left and right brain halves were completely detached but otherwise fully functioning—these people were called split-brain patients. Normally, each side of the brain communicates nonstop with its other half, even as one side or the other takes the lead on certain types of tasks. When the connection was disrupted, however, it became possible to study the job of each side of the brain in isolation. Before having access to this group of patients, scientists knew very little about what the two sides did or how they worked together. For the first time, they could gain insight into the independent functioning of the two sides.

What they found was revolutionary. Their experiments began to reveal the role of the left brain in the storytelling of the thinking mind, the same thinking or analytical mind that invents the powerful story of the self. Gazzaniga's work in the 1960s laid the groundwork for the idea that the self doesn't exist in the way that we think it does.[3] By the 1990s, Gazzaniga himself would be blunt on this topic, starting his book *The Mind's Past* with a chapter titled "The Fictional Self."[4]

It's easy enough to agree that when we are sitting in a café getting to know someone new, we are telling stories. We probably grasp that none of these stories can be completely "true," if for no other reason than that they arise from our subjective experience. We know that stories can change, interpretation matters, and context is key. So, we can accept that even true stories are, at most, a kind of revealing fiction. However, we take for granted that the person telling the story—the "me" sitting across from us—is real. The idea that the self is a fiction seems to defy our very experience. If the "I" telling the story about "me" is not real, what does that mean? Thinking about it for even a few moments can induce a kind of existential vertigo, along with an avalanche of unanswerable questions.

Studying the Split Brain

It is a strange fact that the body is cross-wired: that is, all the input and output from the right half of the body crosses over and is processed by the left brain, and vice versa. To date, science has yet to discover why this is, but it is true for the entire body, and this includes our vision. The left half of what we see is processed by the right side of the brain, and the right half travels to the left side.

Gazzaniga determined that the left side of the brain created explanations and reasons to help make sense of what was going on.[5] The left brain acted as an "interpreter" for reality. However, with the connection between the two halves severed, he could see that the left brain carried on creating stories in ways that were often totally *wrong*. This finding should have rocked the world, but most people haven't even heard of it. To gain a better understanding of how this split brain works, let's look at some of these studies and their findings in more detail.

In one of Gazzaniga's early studies, he showed a split-brain patient a picture of a chicken's foot to the left brain only and a picture of a snow scene to the right brain only. Then, he showed several pictures to both sides of the brain at the same time. The patient was asked which picture was the most related to the original images (the chicken's foot on the left and the snow scene on the right). Each side of the brain performed perfectly: the right brain (using the left hand) pointed to a picture of a snow shovel, whereas the left brain (using the right hand) pointed to a picture of a chicken. Then things got more interesting.

The experimenter asked the patient a simple question: "Why is your left hand pointing to a snow shovel?" Keep in mind, when the experimenter was talking to the split-brain patient, he was talking only to the patient's left brain, because the left brain controls speech. The left brain should have said, "I haven't talked to the right brain in a long time; I don't know why it does what it does with that left hand." But it didn't. Without hesitation, the left brain said, "Oh, that's simple. The chicken foot goes with the chicken, and you need a shovel to clean out the chicken coop." The patient stated this with absolute confidence. Here is what's most important about this: the talking left side of the brain easily came up with a plausible and coherent but *completely incorrect* explanation based on the evidence it had available.

In another example, researchers presented the word *walk* to a patient's right brain only. The patient immediately responded to the request and stood up and started to leave the van in which the test was taking place. When the patient's left brain (language side) was asked why he got up to walk, again the interpreter came up with a plausible but *completely incorrect* explanation: "I'm going into the house to get a Coke." In another exercise, the word *laugh* was presented to the right brain and the patient complied. When asked why she was laughing, her left brain responded by cracking a joke: "You guys come up and test us each month. What a way to make a living!" Remember, the correct answer here would have been, "I laughed because you asked me to."

Think about the significance of this for a moment. The left brain was simply making up interpretations, or stories, for events that were happening in a way that made sense to that side of the brain (a shovel is needed for a chicken coop) or as if it had directed the action (I got up because I needed a drink, or I laughed at my own joke). Neither of these explanations was true, but that was unimportant to the interpretive mind, which was convinced that its explanations were the correct ones.

By studying split brains, researchers have demonstrated the brain's ability and inclination to make up a story that makes sense based on the available information. There's no reason to think that the stories of the self, and the self's preoccupation with sorrows, worries, and problems, are any more than plausible fictions based on incomplete information. Herein lies a powerful opportunity to change our relationship to this fictional self, and work with it to alleviate our suffering and lead happier, more fulfilling lives.

The Mind Likes to Think

You may have heard that the average person has up to sixty thousand thoughts a day, most of which are either repetitive or negative. While it is difficult to authenticate this popular finding, it *feels* believable, which is probably why it is so widespread. In any case, this number seems to validate the overwhelm that most of us feel when it comes to the nonstop processing of the left brain. We spend a huge amount of time in our own mental loops and negative self-talk. We are consumed with anxiety, scanning the horizon for events that may never occur or inflicting self-punishment for events that happened in the past. Furthermore, much of this processing happens unconsciously while we are doing other things.

In fact, research by Harvard scientists Matthew A. Killingsworth and Daniel T. Gilbert shows that much of the time we are not thinking about what we are doing. In their article "A Wandering Mind Is an Unhappy Mind," they show that our mind wanders about 50 percent of our waking day. So, not only do we spend half our lives not living in reality, but this tendency of our minds to wander makes us measurably less happy.[6]

Use the Mind, or It Will Use You

Our goal here is to test the following truth: You are *not* the story in your head, but something much greater (even if you don't know exactly what that is). Let's take a deeper look at the thinking mind, with the hope that the better we understand its functioning, the more we will be able to distance ourselves from the left-brained idea of "self." The mind is like a computer program that borrowed a little from genetics and a little from culture. Part of this program's job is to convince you to identify with its own rules, observations, and impulses. But your true consciousness goes far beyond the confines of this computer program. In my view, the real you is more like the energy that powers the computer.

Let's try to experience, even if only for a few seconds, the clear consciousness I'm talking about via a practice of mindfulness. You've probably heard of mindfulness, as it's become quite popular, though in some ways it is a bit of a misnomer. (A better word might be mind*less*ness.) Let me be clear that one definition of *mind* is the left-brain thinking, processing system that I've been talking about, which is the one we want to see beyond. The other state is more aligned with the right brain, which I've called clear consciousness. This is the state that others often refer to as mindfulness.

Practice: Breathing

A vast range of scientific research now supports what many spiritual systems have taught for millennia: breath holds the power to quiet the thinking mind and opens the door to clear consciousness.[7]

There are innumerable breathing exercises and techniques that can be harnessed to achieve different states of being, but they all rest on the foundational practice of paying attention to (and sometimes manipulating) the breath.

Try the following exercise now, before reading further.

Wherever you are, draw in a long breath. Then slowly let it out. Turn your attention only to the breath. Take another slow breath in. Slowly let it out. When you are done, passively listen to the sounds around you.

Again, I strongly encourage you to do this now, before reading further. You have to experience the practice in order to move beyond the thinking mind. It's not enough to just think about it.

By tuning into the sensation of your breath, even for a brief moment, you have tapped into consciousness beyond the thinking mind. Most people feel at home in the thinking mind. Clear consciousness is a place they rarely visit, and it may even feel frightening or uncomfortable to go there. But if you can access and feel at home in right-brained clear consciousness, it has the power to unleash profound well-being in your everyday life. It is possible to make no self your home and the self a place you sometimes visit.

One way to lessen the influence of the thinking mind is to learn to doubt it. Let's see if your thinking mind is as smart as it tells you it is. . . .

The Left Brain Makes Stuff Up

Your mind is making judgments all day, every day: *This is boring; I ate too much for breakfast; it's cold in here; that guy looks creepy.* . . . They come from seemingly out of nowhere and we have little, if any, control over them. Which judgments pop up, as well as their tone and intensity, will likely depend on your past experiences, your social conditioning, and perhaps even your genetic makeup. But here's something to consider: not only do these judgments seem to arise out of nowhere, the vast majority of them (if not all), are unoriginal. They are more like mirrors of things that someone else said, thought, or felt. So, if none of your thoughts are original, can you even claim them as yours? Is it really you doing the thinking, if you have no control over the thoughts and didn't invent them? This is something the mystics of the East have been espousing for a long time.

While making these judgments and interpretations, the mind is like a fortune-teller, always creating a story to explain what is going to happen and why. Cognitive scientists have studied how the mind first creates a theory about reality and then it attempts to confirm this theory, often ignoring or discrediting any information that would disprove the theory. This is what's referred to as confirmation bias.[8] Let's take a look at how this might happen.

Exercise: What's the Next Number?

What is the next number in this sequence?[9]

2, 4, 6, __ ?

Did you just hear the answer 8, as if from nowhere? Your mind created a theory (the pattern is increasing by two each time) and simply assumed it to be correct. How do you know it's correct if you are only looking to prove it's correct? Perhaps the answer is 4 . . . and then 2, as in 2, 4, 6, 4, 2? Perhaps the pattern is 2, 4, 6, 1000, and the rule is simply that the next number must be larger than the previous one. Notice that when the mind has an idea, it yells out what it believes is a certain answer and then looks for evidence to confirm it. This is what Gazzaniga noticed in his experiments with split-brain patients—the left brain spits out its interpretation based on limited facts, and then believes it without question.

It takes almost no cognitive energy for the left brain to come up with a "right" answer, or a plausible one, and then confirm it. This is often the case with the left brain. Notice as we do each of the following exercises that the answer will often just pop up in your awareness without any effort on your part. In this case, the answer probably came in language form—the word *eight*. Other times, it may come as a picture, or even an emotion or body sensation.

This exercise has been turned into a classroom activity.[10]

Exercise: Why Get Your Glasses?

Joe walks into a restaurant, sits at a booth, and then remembers he left his glasses in the car. He excuses himself to go get them.

> Question: Why does Joe need his glasses?[11] Don't read on until an answer comes to mind.

> *To read the menu* probably just came to mind—or rather *from* the mind.

Next, consider the following: Did you really come up with an answer, or did it just happen without any effort? This is a subtle thing to notice, but the mind has a habit of telling a story to answer any question, or giving an answer based on what it thinks is probable, or past experience (we will revisit the importance of memory in a later chapter).

The correct answer to the question of why this fictional person Joe needs his glasses would be, *My mind doesn't know.* Yet this thought rarely occurs. It would seem strange if it did.

Practice: The "Don't Know" Mind

Perhaps you've heard of the Zen practice called the "don't know" mind. A simple way to get to this "don't know" mind is to consider a question that is impossible to answer, such as this famous example: What is the sound of one hand clapping?

Even as we try to think about this riddle, we can't stop the thinking mind from making automatic assumptions, judgments, and interpretations. However, sitting in the discomfort of a question that has no answer, we can begin to distance ourselves from our own mind. That distance can take the form of bringing in a little bit of uncertainty in the left brain.

If you're having trouble getting started with this practice, you might try asking yourself some more existential questions, which are harder for the mind to answer on autopilot. Ask yourself, *Where do we come from?* Or, *What happens when we die?* These questions are designed to help you get to the "don't know" mind, a place of immediacy in the present moment, where you are no longer depending on the commentary for ready answers.

This can be a very uncomfortable position for the left brain. It may even start screaming at you. If you can, calmly remind yourself that you're not in any danger. Remember to breathe. As you get more comfortable with not knowing, you can apply this practice to the worries that arise in your mind. For example, when you hear the mind say, *I'm worried that XYZ might happen,* you can remind yourself that this mind doesn't know what will happen.

When we open ourselves to not knowing, we begin to experience the world in the present moment as it is, rather than how we are judging or expecting it to be. This can be a subtle difference at first, but it can offer a glimpse beyond the suffering caused by the left brain. When we rest in not knowing, we begin to marvel at the sensations occurring in the moment.

Taken to its extreme, this sense of presence can bring us close to a kind of exquisite existence, in which we are tuned into the greatest of mysteries with every sound, every touch, and every taste. Each experience has the potential to evoke an epiphany of the greatest magnitude. When the mind doesn't know, we can fully appreciate things that most people don't even notice, because they already "know" what the experience is like. You may think living this way is reserved for a few select mystics, saints, or poets, but it's not. You can live there too.

Practice: The Story I'm Making Up

The interpreting mind desperately wants things to make sense and to fit into a story. Life feels easier this way, more predictable, and less painful. We will bend over backward to fill in the blanks that we don't know about a situation in order to bring it to a satisfying conclusion in our minds. We will cast ourselves and others as one-dimensional characters in our story: the hero, the victim, or the villain. From this place, we don't have to feel our feelings or examine what's really going on. We can be right (and righteous) in just the way the left brain loves to be.

The left brain can turn facts into stories at lightning speed. For example, imagine that there are dirty dishes in the sink. The story I tell myself is, *No one does anything in this house except for me!* I'm both a hero and a victim in this tall tale, and I'm feeling righteous. And the moment I believe I am right about this, I am also miserable. Uh-oh.

You can practice framing these fictitious stories and character roles by saying, "The story I'm making up is . . .". It's a simple shift, but it takes some of the defensive edge off. You can do this when you're giving candid feedback to family at home or to colleagues at work. Saying, "The story I'm making up is . . ." creates a space between the self and the truth, and in this way we are using language a little more accurately in terms of describing the world and our place in it. This allows the left brain to be smart and say, *Oh yeah, I know all about stories—they are made up, sometimes they're based on real things, and often there's some metaphor or lesson in them. But they're not real.* Suddenly, the story of your victimhood when it comes to dirty dishes feels a little less raw, and maybe even a little silly. Voilà—you are using the storytelling mind but not believing its hype. You are giving yourself some distance from it.

Exercise: The Left Brain Likes to Follow the Rules

There's another puzzle that reveals the left brain's tendency to make predictions that aren't always right.[12] For this problem, look at the four cards printed on the following page and imagine that they are in front of you. Each card has a number on one side and a letter on the other. The first two cards are letter up, the next two are number up. Your task is to test the following rule: if a card has a D on one side, then it has a 3 on the other.

Which two cards do you flip over to test this rule? Do not read on until you have picked two.

Like most conditioned minds, *D* and *3* probably just popped in your head. The D makes sense because if you turn it over and there is a 3, you have some evidence that the rule works. Your thinking mind then provides an obvious shortcut to confirm this truth: flip over the 3 to see if it has a D on the back.

However, turning over the 3 tells you nothing. If you turn over the 3 and find a G, the rule can still be true, because it only states that if there is a D on one side, then there is a 3 on the other. This is like saying, If Jim cheats on his wife, then he cheats on his taxes. Even if that were true, the reverse may not be—Jim could easily be a romantically faithful tax cheat.

The correct answer to the task is to turn over card 7, as it is the only way to accurately test this rule with the cards provided. If you turn over the 7 and find a D, you can show the rule is false. If you turn it over and find another letter, the rule is still provisionally true.

The left brain isn't great at solving this abstract puzzle, because most of its forty thousand years or so of evolution were focused on more practical matters of survival, like outthinking predators or mistrusting foes. The mind's performance improves when we change the puzzle to something the mind did evolve to solve, like seeing if someone is lying or acting in a dishonest way.

For example, imagine that you are a bar bouncer and you need to make sure no one underage is drinking. Each card represents a customer, with their age on one side and what they are drinking on the other. Just like before, the first two cards show what someone is drinking, while the second two show the age.

Which two cards do you turn over now to make sure no one is drinking underage? I'm guessing that two instantly popped into your awareness, and this time you are correct—or, rather, your mind is correct.

The mind instantly wants to turn over the two correct cards: "Drinking Beer" and "16 Years Old." First "Drinking Beer," to make sure the person's over twenty-one. Next, the mind wants to turn over the "16 Years Old" card to make sure this person is drinking soda and not beer. The "16 Years Old" card is exactly like the 7 in the other problem; your mind's shortcut is just more accurate in this setup.

My hope is that through these simple exercises you can begin to see that the mind isn't as smart as it thinks. Knowing this can feel destabilizing, but it ultimately helps you see beyond the thinking mind, or at least see it as a primitive tool that served our ancestors well in their world but sometimes falls short in our modern world.

Often, those who are most adept at using the left brain's methods to problem solve have the most difficulty letting go of the fiction of the self.

What percentage of the time do you think you are right, or mostly right? Do you think most minds believe they are always right? I would say they do. And yet, if we look at other people's minds and their behaviors, we see clearly that most minds couldn't possibly be right all the time. It's just not likely. It would follow, then, that our minds aren't right most of the time either.

Do you ever question whether your problems are real, or do you only look for evidence to prove that they are? If you think a coworker doesn't like you, do you look for evidence that confirms this or do you try to disprove it? If you make a mistake, do you believe your mind when it tells you that you never do anything right? If the left brain concludes that this is the worst day, week, or year ever, are you ignoring all the evidence that tells you this might not be true?

Exercise: Could the Opposite Be True?

This is a mind-expanding way to approach confirmation bias and call upon the strength of your whole brain. This exercise can also be employed to great effect in groups when people disagree or come up with opposing viewpoints about a problem.

First, physically draw a line in the space you're in. Put down a piece of tape on the floor or designate the edge of the rug as the boundary between one side and the other. Now think of something you believe to be true. Maybe it's something pretty low stakes, like "coffee is healthy to drink." You can probably defend the truth of this statement fairly easily if you believe it. You can go to the internet and do a quick search for "health benefits of coffee" to back up your claim. Physically stand on one side or the other of your line, and go ahead and say out loud or write down five to ten things that support your belief.

Then cross over to the other side of your line.

Now, come up with five to ten reasons the opposite could also be true. You'll need to work harder here to come up with evidence that you find plausible to support the opposite of what you believe. Say these things out loud or write them down. If you're doing this exercise in a group, people should start on whichever side of the line they believe more, and then switch.

Consider the following questions and write about them in a journal:

- How did this exercise change your original beliefs?

- How did it affect the emotional stakes of your problem or disagreement?

- Do you see the problem any differently now?

- Do you see the people who hold opposing beliefs any differently now?

- When you have a strong opinion, are you willing to consider that the opposite could also be true?

Confirmation Bias and the Self

In 1995, McArthur Wheeler decided to rob a few banks in Pittsburgh with a flawless plan, at least to his own mind. Lemon juice is used as invisible ink because it only becomes visible after it is subjected to heat. Therefore, he would rub lemon juice all over his face, making it invisible to the surveillance cameras, and the bank would never be able to record him. Of course, the cameras did record his face and he was quickly caught and put behind bars. Your own thinking mind may immediately dismiss him as "crazy," and that may be true, but it might be more accurate to say that he was experiencing an extreme example of confirmation bias, or believing in an idea and cherry-picking the facts to support it while ignoring those that don't.

In the late 1990s, the now-infamous Heaven's Gate cult made headlines when thirty-nine people were found to have committed mass suicide based on their collective belief that a spaceship was traveling behind the Comet Hale-Bopp that was passing by Earth, and that this spaceship would take true believers to a better place. Before this terrible tragedy, however, some of the group members put their money together to buy a high-quality telescope in order to take a closer look at the spaceship itself. Of course, they were unable to see it; however, after having failed to confirm their belief with their own eyes, they concluded that the telescope was in fact defective and asked for a refund. After all, it had to be the telescope's fault; it couldn't be that they were wrong.

One of the left brain's most powerful desires is to seek out consistency. Consistency is the bedrock of predictability, and the left brain wants to keep us safe by predicting possible outcomes. The brain will work overtime, and in total defiance of reality, to keep consistency between what we think, what we do, and how we feel. To this end, we steadfastly avoid the experience of being inconsistent in our feelings, thoughts, and actions. This inconsistency creates what we call cognitive dissonance.

Cognitive dissonance literally means the pain we experience if our thoughts, behaviors, and emotions are out of alignment. This pain can be physical, emotional, mental, or all three. The term was coined by Leon Festinger in the 1950s, and more than three thousand experiments since have elucidated what it is and how it works. Cognitive dissonance accounts for why it is so hard to leave a relationship we've invested in. The mind has watched us do something for a long time, and the idea that we have made a mistake is taxing and painful. After all, each of us believes that our mind is right most of the time. So while the Heaven's Gate telescope story may sound outrageous, the behavior of those cult members isn't very far removed from the average acrobatics our own minds perform many times a day to keep us from experiencing the intense discomfort of cognitive dissonance. It's easier for the thinking mind to create elaborate explanations to justify a decision rather than simply admit a mistake. In a similar way, the left brain avoids thinking or admitting we are wrong in order to avoid cognitive dissonance. We believe we are smart, and most of our decisions are good, so we must also be right. Finding out we're wrong can cause actual pain as we try to hold on to our view of ourselves.

Exercise: Better Than Average

Western culture particularly values the thinking mind. We draw a line from ancient Greek philosophers, through the Enlightenment, all the way to being "smart" thinkers who can know facts and solve problems. Of course, confirmation bias multiplies whatever we think. When you only look for evidence to prove an idea, it makes the idea very believable. Furthermore, being aware of confirmation bias has been demonstrated to make us even *more* susceptible to it! We convince ourselves that we are weighing alternate viewpoints, and our original belief becomes even stronger.

Below are three attributes you might find discussed on a typical self-reflection survey. At this point, your thinking mind might be skeptical about these "tricky" exercises, but try to be honest with your response if you really want to get the most from this book. Simply make a check on the line where you believe you fall for each category.

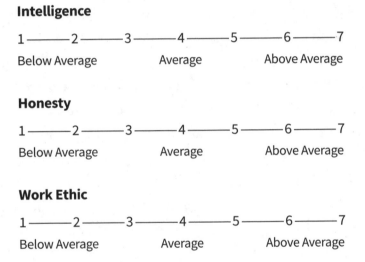

Intelligence

1 —— 2 —— 3 —— 4 —— 5 —— 6 —— 7

Below Average   Average   Above Average

Honesty

1 —— 2 —— 3 —— 4 —— 5 —— 6 —— 7

Below Average   Average   Above Average

Work Ethic

1 —— 2 —— 3 —— 4 —— 5 —— 6 —— 7

Below Average   Average   Above Average

Of course, I have no idea where you really fall on any of these dimensions, but it shouldn't surprise you to learn that each mind will overestimate where it thinks it falls, and most will be just a little above average. The mind will not allow itself to exaggerate too much, as that would be arrogant, but it will typically judge itself just a little above the curve.

Yet of course if we looked at the whole population, it's not possible that everyone can be just a little above average. What is most telling about this is how predictable most minds are in considering themselves a little above average. This tells us less about anyone's actual relationship to average, and more about the universal impulse to push away from cognitive dissonance and find that comfortable sweet spot of "a little better than everyone else." Of course, most of us know that truly getting better at something requires accepting discomfort.

Motivated Reasoning

The left brain is so predictable that numerous studies have shown how its ability to reason depends largely on what we stand to gain or lose from the evaluation at hand. For example, imagine your task is to find flaws in a research article. The article reviews research that concludes that drinking coffee is strongly related to breast cancer. From the list below, which group of people do you think will find the most flaws in the research?

- males who do not drink coffee

- females who do not drink coffee

- males who drink coffee

- females who drink coffee

If you picked the last one, you are correct. Female coffee drinkers have something to lose if the research is correct. The reasoning of this group was highly motivated to avoid the discomfort of believing in a direct link between coffee drinking and cancer.

For those of you who are female coffee drinkers, don't worry—this research was made up for the study. The mind likes to think that it is rational and logical, but the facts show it simply isn't a lot of the time.[13]

Here's a question to consider, and it might ignite some cognitive dissonance for you: Is it possible that confirmation bias could also be at play when the mind looks for, and creates, a sense of self? How can we expect the mind to behave rationally in this area when it doesn't do so in any other area when self-interest is at stake?

Putting on a Mask

Masks hold a fascinating place in every human culture and history, and very effectively expose and illuminate the idea of the fictional/true self, whether for purposes of entertainment, spiritual exploration, education, or healing.

In the Italian performance tradition of *commedia dell'arte*, there are set archetypal characters that actors have played for centuries. These include a lecherous old man called Pantalone, a trickster servant called Arlecchino, and a wide-eyed fool, Zanni, among others. Each character has a specific mask they wear, a half mask that covers only from the top of the forehead to the bottom of the nose, leaving the mouth exposed.

An actor playing any of these characters has a precise ritual to working with these masks. They begin by holding the mask up to their own face, looking at it as if in a mirror. First, they will see it as an object, just a mask. The actor will continue to look into the empty "eyes" of the mask until they get the distinct feeling that the mask is *looking back at them*. As soon as this happens, they can turn the mask around and put it on their own face, seeing out of these new eyes of the character.

In fact, we probably perceive masks with the face-processing center located in the right brain, a small area called the fusiform gyrus that only processes faces. The mask taps into a right-brained, ancient understanding of personhood, one that knows that any "self" is only a mask we wear to play within our given reality. With the mask now on, the individual self recedes into a collective understanding of an archetype, in service to a different goal—to make us laugh, cry, escape, or understand ourselves and each other more deeply.

Practice: Pretend to Be Another Self

If you have access to a mask, you can also play with this ritual of looking into its eyes until you feel it looking at you, and then putting it on and experiencing the world through the mask's eyes.

But we also wear the "mask" of our individual identity in many other ways, including our clothing and accessories. This is a silly exercise that your left brain is going to try to convince you not to do. Do it anyway. Go to a thrift store (or just rummage through family members' closets) for items of clothing that you would never ordinarily wear. Pick out glasses you don't need, shoes that don't fit, hats that look strange, colors and patterns that don't match or you never normally wear.

Put on the costume of this different self, and follow its lead to do what this self wants you to do. Get a snack as this self; pick out a book to read or music to listen to as this self; look in the mirror and say hello to this self. If you're feeling brave enough, go outside for a walk as this self.

After you've done this, write down some of your feelings and anything you learned in your journal. Here are a few questions to help you get started:

- Do you think you were being "you"? If not, who were you?

- What new impulses or desires did you experience?

- Do you feel energized? Exhausted? Strange?

- How did others react to you in this self? Was this uncomfortable, or fun?

- Could it be that you wear a mask or costume every day, and you have simply mistaken this for your true self?

Overcoming Left-Brain Laziness with Logic and Awareness

The mind has a certain built-in laziness. In the same way that water will follow the path of least resistance, the mind will follow paths that require the least amount of effort. This isn't a problem; it's just the evolutionary design of the brain, which had to conserve energy and prioritize survival. In modern times, however, we sometimes will want to overcome this inner inertia so that we can get more out of our circumstances and our own thinking capacity. We're in a privileged position, evolutionarily speaking, and we can use the vast powers of our minds to become happier, more productive, and more connected.

First, let's take a look at some of the classic ways the mind prefers to stay lazy.

Exercise: Welcome to Your Lazy Mind

Consider the following argument and decide if it is valid. To be valid, the third statement must necessarily follow from the first two statements. It doesn't matter what A and B and C stand for—they can stand for anything—but no matter what you put in, the conclusion must follow from the first two statements every time.

1. Some A are B.

2. Some B are C.

3. Therefore, some A are C.

Circle your answer:

- Yes, it's valid.

- No, it's not valid.

The mind is predictable. You probably heard the voice in your head again, and it confidently stated *Yes, this is valid*. However, if we replace these abstract letters with concrete examples from the real world, we see the mind is again wrong. Let's replace A with "tall people," B with "rich people," and C with "short people" and take another look.

1. Some tall people are rich.

2. Some rich people are short.

3. Therefore, some tall people are short people.[14]

Here's another example.[15] Jack is looking at Anne, but Anne is looking at George. Jack is married, but George is not. Is a married person looking at an unmarried person? Don't read on until you mark your answer.

A. Yes

B. No

C. Cannot be determined

If you are like my students, the mind probably glanced over the problem and then decided C. The answer is A, but in order to reach that answer the mind must do something it dreads—work a little. The mind must ponder two possible situations, which takes both time and energy. Let's take the extra time to consider both options here:

1. If Anne is married, then a married person (Anne) is looking at an unmarried person (George).

2. If Anne is unmarried, then a married person (Jack) is looking at an unmarried person (Anne).

In either case, then, the statement "a married person is looking at an unmarried person" is true.[16]

For this exercise, imagine that you are a new doctor and a patient has just tested positive for a rare disease. It is so rare that only one in one thousand people get it. Now, no test is perfect; in fact, this test has a 5 percent false positive rate. This means that five times out of one hundred, it will turn up positive when in fact the person doesn't have the disease. What are the odds that your patient truly has the disease?

A. There is a 95 percent chance the patient has the disease.

B. There is a 50 percent chance the patient has the disease.

C. There is a 2 percent chance the patient has the disease.

The voice in your head probably just yelled out *95 percent*, perhaps even following up with a little of "reasoning" that went something like this: *Well, if the test is wrong 5 percent of the time, it must be right 95 percent of the time.* The mind didn't know what to do with what's called the base rate. That is, how often the disease exists in the population. The mind evolved in small groups of around a hundred to one hundred and fifty people, so it doesn't know how to factor in larger numbers like one in one thousand. To get the correct answer, you must consider what would happen if you tested one thousand people. If you tested one thousand people, only one would really have the disease, but fifty more would test positive because fifty is 5 percent of one thousand. So, out of one thousand people fifty-one people would test positive. Out of the fifty-one people who all tested positive, what are the odds your patient is the one with the disease? The correct statistic is one in fifty-one, or about 2 percent ($1/52$). The mind thought it would be 95 percent, but the true answer is only 2 percent.[17]

If your mind started to wander while reading this, it is because the brain is too lazy to read exactly why it is wrong, especially because you have no personal motivation to be right about this puzzle, and no consequences if you are wrong. It feels better to save the energy and avoid discomfort.

In each of the previous puzzles, we see the left brain's resistance to using extra energy to define and solve logic-based problems.

And in all three cases, the logic was simple in the end. So one strategy that we can all use to counteract the lazy left brain is to build in a way to make sure we are activating sound logic.

Practice: Three Ways to Access Better Logic

The problems above have no meaning for any of us—they're just abstract thought experiments. But there are plenty of problems and decisions we make in our real lives that would benefit from the same kind of sound logic that the left brain loves to sidestep and avoid. How can we evaluate competing offers of a home or car loan? How do we help our kids decide which college to apply to?

Put a Price on It

If being wrong costs something, or if you get a bonus for being right, your left brain will invest more energy in being right. What if you had to send fifty dollars to a charity whose mission statement you despised if you got any of the above questions wrong? You would definitely take more time on your responses!

Call a Friend

Inside the echo chamber of our own heads, it's very easy to be certain that we are right. When it comes to decision making, it can be a good idea to call on a friend you trust and ask them to be candid with you. They will see patterns in your thinking and behavior that you are blind to. It may also be helpful to talk to someone who isn't a friend. Try asking a stranger, or perhaps someone who seems so different from you it would almost seem crazy to ask for their opinion.

Teach It to Someone Else

We can read a book or watch a video and think we understand something, but this is often a hidden way that the left brain conserves energy. *I got it, let's move on,* it seems to say. Teaching what we think we know to others is a more complex cognitive task. It makes us think more deeply, face questions about our views, and look at the problem from multiple angles. It also adds positive social pressure to the mix. We want to do a good job in the eyes of others.

Informal Fallacies

One of my favorite topics to teach about the left brain is its tendency to fall for informal fallacies. These are situations wherein the content of an argument is flawed, but the mind falls for it regardless, coming up with a flawed solution or answer that feels right.

Exercise: The Person or the Argument?

Consider the following questions.

- Would you go to a couples' therapist who has been divorced five times?

- Would you listen to a lecture about the dangers of drugs from a current drug user?

- Imagine that your doctor smokes, drinks, and is totally out of shape. Would you listen to their advice on living a healthy lifestyle?

An *ad hominem* argument is an informal fallacy in which a person is attacked rather than an argument itself. It is Latin and translates as "argument against the person." If you want to mislead someone or a group of people, an ad hominem argument is extremely effective because it relies on our left brain's tendency to want to reduce an individual with a complex set of talents and flaws into a more manageable cognitive label. It also taps into our most basic beliefs as social creatures about trust and interpersonal connections.

We are all, in different ways, saints and sinners—sometimes even on the same day! But the mind would rather deal with one label per person, rather than taking the extra effort to compartmentalize conflicting individual talents and flaws. Because of this, the mind cannot or simply does not separate the message from the messenger.

Consider someone who your mind has put into a simple mental box as "a jerk" or "lazy" or any other label. The simplicity of this label colors your view of whatever they say whether it's an oft-divorced therapist or an unhealthy doctor. As it turns out, this tendency to equate the messenger with the message also provides a shortcut for attacking a given position or argument. The mind is equally persuaded by an attack on the person as it is by an attack on the actual argument or evidence itself because it can't separate the two. This is likely why so much of politics is centered on name-calling and personal attacks. It's an effective tactic aimed at minds that can't separate message from messenger. In one study, subjects had to evaluate a scientific paper and were shown arguments against the contents of the paper as well as personal attacks on the scientists who wrote it. The results demonstrated that personally attacking the scientists was just as effective as attacking the actual research.[18]

In the same way that the past does not define the present, the messenger does not define the message. It is perfectly possible that an antidrug message is sound, regardless of who gives the lecture. It is possible that even if a therapist has divorced countless times, their therapy is still sound. It is possible that a CEO could run a company very well even if they cheated on their spouse. The world is infinitely more complex, layered, and contradictory than simple left-brain categories allow, but most of us don't appreciate this.

As you continue to do these exercises, you might find yourself marveling at the illusory nature of categories. It may seem strange that you ever thought these categories were real things.

Awareness

You probably noticed that in each of the examples and exercises so far, your initial instinctual answer was false. It wasn't too hard to find the right answer. All it took was urging the lazy mind to become a little more aware, to go a little deeper, and to use resources just beyond the grasp of the thinking mind.

One of these recourses is awareness, something that is integrally connected to the present moment, and therefore the right brain. Awareness can be described as the experience of the witness or the observer of what is happening now.

In fact, this awareness is a reliable antidote to the laziness the mind is apt to return to as it tries to conserve caloric energy and avoid the emotional and physical pain of cognitive dissonance. Awareness, it turns out, is an essential key in our quest to tip the balance from over-reliance on our thinking mind to feeling at ease within clear consciousness. The Buddha told us this too.

Practice: Strengthen Your Awareness

It might seem strange, but tuning into our physical body can be a great way to increase our mental capabilities. This is a basic body scan practice that you can use whenever you want to gain deeper insight about a problem or decision. It will also help you create some distance between your left brain and the problem.

Start in a seated position with your feet firmly on the floor and your back resting upright and comfortably in a chair.

Take three deep breaths, in through the nose and out through the mouth, releasing tension with a deep sigh on the exhale. This breathing pattern clears out the lungs and lessens the feelings of stress in the body.

Now, turn your awareness inside your body, starting with your feet. Feel any pressure, tension, or temperature sensations. You might imagine a liquid or glowing light filling your body, traveling up through your ankles, calves, knees, thighs, and into your groin. Keep breathing as you experience whatever is going on in your body. If you find yourself telling a story about it, acknowledge the story and then let it go, returning to awareness of breath and sensation. Work your way up your body, down your arms to your fingertips, up through your neck and out the top of your head.

This kind of body awareness is exactly the kind of thing that the lazy left brain doesn't think is worth the time or energy it takes to do, even though it can be done sitting still in just a few minutes. And yet whenever you do it, you immediately feel more centered, more curious, and more alive.

- How did it feel to be conscious without thinking?

- Where did all of your problems go while you were simply aware of the body?

- Did your left brain keep chattering, or did its volume and intensity drop down a little?[19]

The Left Brain Gets Fooled, the Right Brain Gets Wise

You've probably heard the saying, "I'll believe it when I see it." But the reverse is also true: "I'll see it when I believe it." That's because, in a scientifically substantiated way, we really do see what we believe. Our thinking mind has programmed our senses to view the world in a particular way. On occasion, this program results in illusions and mistakes. Furthermore, even if we intellectually know these are mistakes, the mind is still programmed to see what it believes. Our intellectual understanding cannot override this. This might be even more clear if we move from the stories the mind tells us through language into the complexities of visual understanding.

Visual illusions are another way to explore the mind's problem solving, and the same mechanisms are at work. The mind will make certain assumptions and come to certain conclusions and all you can do is sit back and watch. You can even show the mind how it is wrong and it will have no influence on the illusion—you can't "unsee" the illusion.

Exercise: The Mind Believes What It Sees

Let's start with the Ponzo illusion. Which line looks the longest?

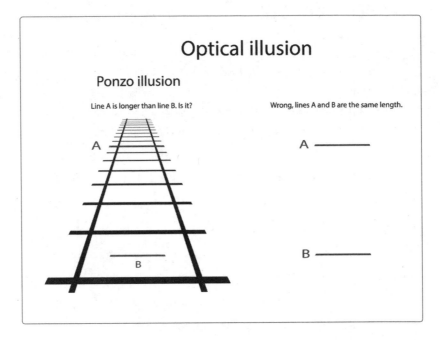

I like this one because it seems so obvious. It really appears as if the upper line is much bigger than the other, but they are all the same size. Prove this to your mind by measuring each line. They are all the same. Now, sit back and see if the mind learned from this. I've taught this for twenty years, and to my mind the upper line still seems longer.

Drawing on the Right Side of the Brain

Dr. Betty Edwards's groundbreaking 1979 book *Drawing on the Right Side of the Brain* codified an elegant method of learning to make realistic drawings by harnessing the right brain's powers of visual perception.[20] Her teachings are based on the work of Roger W. Sperry, the neuroscientist who worked with Gazzaniga and split-brain patients to understand the interdependent and separate functions of the left and right brain hemispheres.

Edwards found that the basic skill of learning to draw also teaches us to make the mental shift from left-brain thinking, which is so dominant in our culture, to right-brain thinking. This leads to more creative, connected, intuitive thinking and problem solving across all disciplines, not just in the visual arts.

Edwards's great insight is that the left brain can't be talked out of participating in a task that would be better accomplished with the right brain. Take the example of drawing a self-portrait. For someone not trained to use their brain as an artist does, looking in a mirror and sketching your own face probably results in line drawings that stand in for the shapes of the nose, mouth, eyes, and forehead but look nothing like the image in the mirror, which has an infinite amount of detail, shading, and depth. This is because the left brain chatters away, naming and categorizing the features of the face, pushing out the more accurate nonverbal understandings of the right brain.

Edwards's rule for drawing, then, is that "In order to gain access to sub-dominant, somewhat hard-to-access R-mode, the non-verbal, visual perceptual system of the brain, it is necessary to present one's own brain with a task that the dominant verbal system, L-mode, will turn down."[21] Basically, the left brain has to say, *No thank you! I don't do that!* so that the more talented right brain can step in.

Exercise: Draw Your Room

Look around the room you're in right now and examine the angles of the various lines that make up the connections between walls, floor, and ceiling. Try drawing these using the left side of the brain, really thinking about the name for each part of the room as you draw it. Then take a look at your work. You've probably drawn horizontal and vertical lines to represent the spaces and shapes in your room. The left brain "knows" that the ceiling is a horizontal line and parallel to the floor on all sides. Does this look like your room?

Next, try making a new drawing, and this time tell yourself to just copy the angles of the lines as you see them, even if they are "wrong." Put a little space between what you are doing and the words "ceiling," "floor," and "wall." Your left brain will quickly give up: *I know that ceilings are perpendicular to walls, so I'm not going to participate in this ridiculous exercise.* You will probably find that this drawing much more closely resembles the room you are actually seeing.

Exercise: Upside Down Drawing

This exercise is one of Edwards's most basic ways to bypass the left brain. Print out a picture or a realistic drawing of a face. Place it next to your empty paper and copy the drawing as best you can. Your left brain will happily get involved, telling you how a beard looks, or that eyeglasses are perfectly symmetrical.

Next, turn the printed image upside down and make a new drawing. The left brain will almost always step back quickly, because it has little use for naming and categorizing upside-down things in normal life. As the left brain quiets, the right brain can step in and direct the hand to draw the lines as they really are. When you're finished, turn your drawing right side up and marvel at the difference between your first drawing and your second one.

Attention

Our thinking mind has evolved certain ways of paying attention and has a host of ready shortcuts in this area. We are hypervigilant for signs of danger, including the social dangers of humiliation or shame. Our attention operates nonstop on an instinctual level, guided by the thinking mind.

Exercise: What Draws the Eye

Our first exercise with attention will be a short demonstration on the next page. Simply turn the page.

Then you will read this.

First you will read this!

You will read this last.

Attention guides our senses to select some parts of our environment over others. It is guided by physical cues such as size, color, contrast, and placement. It is amplified and sharpened by contexts of culture, history, and emotions. If one knows the rules (advertisers know them well), your mind's attention can be easily manipulated in the same way that any other aspect of the mind can be manipulated.

However, you can also become the observer of your attention, and notice how your attention is pushed in this direction and pulled in another. When you are the conscious witness to attention, you are no longer caught up in the mechanics of mind.

In the same way that you can use awareness to observe your thoughts, you can also begin to notice your shifts in attention. In the same way that your eyes move across a picture looking for something interesting, unusual, or attractive, your mind scans your environment. Some things light up our attention more than others, like a spotlight on a tapdancing performer, or an advertisement that brightens our view like a tree in full bloom. Rather than being dragged around by attention, we can learn to step back and become the observer not only of our environment but of the very way that our attention interacts with it.

Practice: Become the Observer of Attention

This simple practice can help you notice where attention goes and what it is attracted to.

Close your eyes for a moment, and then open them and take note of what catches your attention. List the top three things you notice, whether they are the first things you see or the most arresting:

1.

2.

3.

Why do you think you noticed these items over others? If we are hungry, we notice food; if we are thirsty, we notice something to drink. Our thinking mind has also been programmed to notice all sorts of things we are supposed to be interested in.

- Did you see the entire space or just a few items that you think are important?

- Did you notice something "wrong," like a scratch on the floor or unwashed dishes?

- Were you more drawn to the living things in your space or to inanimate objects?

No answer is right or wrong. You're simply practicing the art of noticing.

Attention isn't just what we notice—it's also what we *don't* notice. It is obviously easy to notice what we are noticing; it is more difficult to start paying attention to what we have missed because we never noticed it in the first place.

Practice: Noticing the Unnoticed

You surely know that there is a world out there that you've never noticed, but you might not realize how close it is to you. This is because there's an essential difference in how the two sides of your brain pay attention. The right brain keeps the big picture in focus and attends to a wider array of input. The left brain, on the other hand, maintains a kind of spotlight of focus on one thing at a time, intense and narrow. When we rely on the left brain, we can miss much of what is right under our nose.[22]

In practicing meditation, there's a good reason it is so common to start by paying attention to the breath. Breathing is one of the processes that is both programmed and also can come under our conscious control. Attention is very similar. Our attention can wander, running on autopilot, or we can learn to guide it, sustain it, and use it in a purposeful way.

Here are a few simple ways to work with attention to reveal things you've never noticed before.

The next time you're at the bookstore or the library, go to a section you've never been in before. Pick up a magazine or a book and flip to a random page without an advertisement (ads are designed to catch the attention of the left brain in most cases, so avoid those for this practice). Take a breath and count three things you notice.

The thinking mind often latches on to a game or a goal, so you can also challenge yourself to notice new things. I've taken a jog down the same street for over ten years now and notice something new every time I look for something new.

One of the simplest ways to tap into expanded attention is to enlist the help of someone else to do some noticing together. Walking around a new neighborhood, or visiting a forest, a beach, or a museum with a child or someone older than you can reveal all sorts of unnoticed details. Even sitting down next to or taking a walk with a pet and noticing what they seem to be noticing could reveal new information.

This practice never gets old, as you will continue to notice more and more and start to wonder how you ever missed all of this before.

Are You a Weirdo?

The origins of the word *weird* are themselves rather weird. It can be traced back to the word *wyrd*, whose meaning is less about being a strange outsider and more associated with fate, perhaps even going back to a goddess who controlled human destiny. What if it is our destiny to be weird?

Conformity to the group may be part of the left brain's modus operandi, but something motivates us to be different too. There is something enticing and freeing about expressing our inner weirdness, which has long been a hallmark of artists and creators. In this way, letting our weirdness out can be another tool to access our right brain, moving beyond the left brain's limited illusion of self.

Remember, you have the freedom to embrace your weirdness and to follow your own path, which need not be confined by the limitations and rules of the problem-solving left brain. I encourage you to follow the weirdness of your path into deeper, murkier, more fertile territory.

One powerful way to expose the left brain's limitations and release your bondage to social conformity is to practice being different. Let your weirdness out.

Practice: Let Your Weirdness Out

Go somewhere that no one goes, like an alleyway or the forgotten corner of a cemetery. Or go somewhere that lots of people go but do something different there (for example, bring a book to an amusement park, draw in a sketchbook at church, or dance in a public square). Go barefoot. Climb a tree. When everyone is sitting but you feel like standing, stand. Make up a song or a poem and sing it out loud. Rediscover a retro trend and enjoy bringing it back. Wear colors that don't "go together." (All colors go together.) Dig out something you love from your closet that you never wear and put it on.

Remember, you only think you know what others are thinking. Perhaps, rather than making fun of you, they will envy your weirdness and your courage to express your individuality. Plus, even if they *are* thinking negative thoughts about you, these thoughts aren't even coming from who they truly are. It is just a program in their head controlling who they think they are, producing judgmental thoughts that they have little control over.

Abstractions and Categories

The word *abstract* comes from the Latin *abstractus,* meaning "to detach." With abstract thinking, we detach from the physical reality of the world by conceptualizing it into thought. The left brain excels at making the real an abstraction, not to mention that the illusory self it creates is ultimately an abstraction too. The left brain spends an enormous amount of its time translating the real world into abstract mental boxes of its own creation, and often gets carried away in the process.

What do I mean by a "mental box"? In cognitive science, we call these mental boxes *categories.*[23] The thinking mind, specifically the left brain, creates categories out of things it believes go together. Categorization is considered a core cognitive skill, and the left brain can categorize things according to a single shared feature or quality, or many. Categories can overlap, and they can exclude or include similarities and differences. For example, everyone who uses their left hand to write might be included in a group of left-handers. It doesn't matter if you are tall, short, young, or old—every other quality is ignored in favor of the single feature that creates the group. To believe in categories, you must ignore a lot and pay attention to only a little.

All humans are born with the ability to categorize, but the way we form categories is learned and heavily influenced by cultural input. While other species can categorize, humans excel in this ability just as humans excel at language. In fact, categories are an essential part of language.

Just as the thinking mind makes things up, our spectacular ability to categorize comes with certain problems and oddities. For example, categories allow us to think in strange ways. We can easily put a tarantula and a kitten in the same mental box of "pets," even if the two share very few other qualities (and many people would prefer a cat as a pet to a spider). We know that dogs are different than cats, but we also know that a dog can be a pet or a police officer or both. The mind is so good at creating categories that most people live in categorical worlds of their own creation and are not even aware of this because it happens so easily.

Because of this we can say that when we first started to think is also the moment we began to trade reality for a thought about reality, a mental representation or abstraction of reality. Without abstraction, we wouldn't be able to categorize. While the benefits of using categories are clear, in many ways these categories have worked so well that we've forgotten they are mental fictions. The categories have become our reality.

Exercise: Judging a Book by Its Cover

Consider the next situation and choose either A or B. Jim is thirty and introverted. As a student, Jim was an avid reader who often got lost in his inner world. Is Jim more likely to be a bank teller, or a bank teller who enjoys poetry? Circle one before you continue.

A. A bank teller

B. A bank teller who enjoys poetry

Let me guess, you heard a voice in your head that confidently said B. But let's ask the thinking mind to go a little deeper. Imagine all the bank tellers in the world contained within an imaginary circle. Now imagine a subset, a smaller circle, that would represent bank tellers who also enjoy poetry. Statistically, B is far less likely because it is more restrictive and must fulfill two requirements whereas A only requires one. The mind was also drawn to picking B because of its sense that within the general population, people who are introverts (one category) and had been avid readers in school (a smaller category within "introverts") would be more likely to also be people who enjoy poetry (yet a smaller category within introverted, avid student readers). In fact, statistically, Jim has more chance of being a bank teller than he has of being a bank teller *and* possessing any other quality. So the answer is A.[24]

Perhaps a bodybuilder comes to interview for a job at your bookstore, and in your head you sarcastically hear, *I bet this guy reads a lot of books.* This is the categorizing habit of the thinking mind. There is nothing to feel guilty about as long as you don't act on it. Perhaps you can even learn to laugh at how silly the mind can be and remind yourself that this is an individual, not the box your mind put them in. Perhaps you can bring awareness to your learned rules of categorization and follow the thread to unravel how these categories play out in culture, law, education, and economic realities in your given context. In reality, you know nothing about this person except what you are learning in the here and now. We only need to look for uniqueness. This is seeing beyond the illusion of categorization. In fact, we could say that the no-self experience, or what we've been calling clear consciousness, is the experience of being in reality without categories.

There are many ways in which individuals are currently categorized, most obviously age, race, gender expression, nationality, class, sexual orientation, and many more. There are countless other ways they *could* be categorized (finger length, shoe size, tendency to laugh), but for whatever reasons these are not the defining characteristics of our main cultural stereotypes. (Hint: Follow the influence, money, and power at stake to understand more about why a stereotyped group is singled out for any given reason. Remember how we learned the bias of the thinking mind when its own interests are at stake.)

When we categorize a person into any group, we are doing some serious abstract thinking. We are literally leaving reality and entering a world of thoughts and mentally constructed boxes. Yet these boxes dictate a host of real-world consequences. They are codified into cultural norms and legal statutes and play out in violence, inequality, and preferential treatment. Why do we do all this when any given group exists nowhere else except in the thinking mind? Because we equate the thinking mind's abstractions with reality.

Society can't seem to eradicate stereotypes. In fact, the more we try, the more we end up doing exactly what we are trying *not* to do. Just as our efforts to overcome confirmation bias can leave us more susceptible to it, our focus on fixing problematic categorizations can lead us down a confusing path of labels and behaviors that only reinforce its harmful effects. You can't think your way out of a thinking problem. I often wonder if our overidentification with the mind as reality is the main culprit here. Identify with the thinking mind and you are subject to all its mechanisms and preferences for the abstract over reality, including representativeness. Taking a step back, we can quickly see that these categories bear little resemblance to the people and things they are meant to be standing for.

Exercise: Still Judging a Book by Its Cover

I want to draw your attention to the stubbornly persistent influence of the thinking mind. Even after the mind has learned everything in this book, it will still respond with similar answers to the same kinds of puzzles. (This was true of visual illusions, as you might remember.) The best we can do is accept this is the truth of how the thinking mind works and bring awareness and curiosity about whether the voice in your head might be telling you the wrong answer.

Here's one example. Zoe listens to new age music, practices yoga and aromatherapy, and enjoys discussing spirituality with her friends. Is Zoe more likely to be

A. A medical doctor

B. An energy healer

The mind assumes that Zoe must be an energy healer, desperate to lump "energy healer" in the same category as new age music and aromatherapy. This "feels right" as the mind seeks to confirm the general or abstract rule rather than the individual exception. But it can't be correct that Zoe is more likely to be an energy healer than a doctor. The simple fact that there are far more medical doctors than energy healers in the world means that it is far more likely that Zoe is a medical doctor.

Steven Pinker is arguably one of the most influential cognitive scientists working today. Pinker has made an emphatic point that one cannot make reliable judgments about the individual from their group membership. Simply because a person may identify as male does not mean he will always be physically strong. Simply identifying as female does not mean that an individual will necessarily be compassionate or caring. The "truth" of certain abstract averages within categories simply doesn't apply reliably to the individuals within these groups.

Some cognitive scientists have argued that the mind's purpose is to simplify a complex world. It separates the world into abstract groups based on very limited information. But much of human history consists of wars and battles that have been fought over the way the mind created these groups. Our wars and even office politics are the outcome of this programing. The groups that are fighting are not even real; they are abstractions of the mind.

Practice: How Patriotic Are You?

One category that is completely abstract is that which we call countries. There are 142 countries in the world today, all of which are made up by arbitrary lines on a map, and only exist in the mind. People have died over these lines, of course. While I am not denigrating the sacrifices made so that we can live in a free society, I do think it's equally important to recognize the dangers of this abstract thinking when we judge others as "enemies" based on these arbitrary lines. Consider this the next time you are someplace and a flag is honored or the pledge of allegiance is recited. What does that mean for you and why?

One of the most powerful possibilities of fully appreciating the next cognitive revolution is our ability to become aware of this categorization habit and to realize that it isn't indicative of who we truly are in any way, shape, or form. None of us are really in any of these groups; the mind only thinks it is so. Categories are the last major obstacle in our quest to overcome the illusion of self, and unlearning our reliance on them is difficult work. It's important not to judge ourselves or be discouraged when we can't let go of them right away, or when we slip back into believing in them.

Irrational Phobias and Superstitions

The mind makes connections that it hopes will predict the future, but many times these are as far off track as the conclusions of the split-brain patients we discussed earlier. One persistent theory on the internet, for example, is that the number of movies that Nicolas Cage has made in any given year perfectly correlates to how many people drowned in a certain pool that same year. From this, one could imagine someone protesting that Cage stop making films to save people from drowning. It speaks to a favorite pastime of the mind to stick strange things in the same mental box. More often than not, this tendency to make false connections is a source of suffering, and is commonly called superstition.

Black cats, ladders, broken mirrors, Friday the thirteenth . . . the cultural left brain has made all sorts of false connections out of everyday fears. Our sympathetic nervous system is wired for fear, helping protect our ancestors when danger from predators was common and being cast out from the group meant certain death. Fortunately, most of us no longer need to watch for attacks from lions, tigers, or bears. And we have much broader access to social acceptance than membership in a single hunter-gatherer clan. Despite this, mortal fear still churns through us on a regular basis. Sometimes, this fear gets channeled into irrational fears and superstitions by the thinking mind.

While superstitions about black cats and Nicolas Cage films are easy to spot, others can be more subtle. This is especially true when they are created by religious, political, or cultural thought patterns. We might be told that "everything happens for a reason," a kind of superstitious wash that attempts to explain away complexity and pain. We might be conditioned to expect that something bad will happen after a string of good fortune. Sometimes our whole value system has a superstitious aspect, almost as if a bearded guy in a red suit is keeping tabs on our good and bad deeds from his home in the North Pole.

Don Miguel Ruiz, shaman and author of *The Four Agreements*, said at an event in Sedona, Arizona, "The time for superstition is over . . . the truth is that we are all God." I'm quite sure he didn't mean this in the egoic sense of the little self created by the thinking mind, which he also teaches is an illusion. Rather, he was describing that our true selves are more akin to clear consciousness, the one life that many call God or universal good.

To lessen the suffering in our own lives, we can start to notice when we participate in superstitions, and we can try to make right connections instead. Of course, the interesting thing about superstitions is that they are resistant to change. That is, even if you know they are silly, the mind still believes in them and reacts to them, believing something like, "It's better to be safe than sorry."

Practice: Don't Believe Everything You Think

Find a judgmental thought that you often have, one that feels true but also causes suffering when you think it. Some common ones are *I'm such a failure, I shouldn't have gotten divorced,* or *I shouldn't have quit that job.* (Remember, there are virtually no original thoughts here.)

Next, I invite you to remember that thoughts are not facts. They are judgments, which are by definition categorical opinions.

We can even test if that thought is unequivocally true. This is similar to how we approached debunking some of the visual illusions earlier in this book. Even though one line really looks longer than the other, we can get a ruler and build evidence. There's no equivalent to a ruler for measuring the truth of our thoughts, but there are a few other things we can do to question their validity.

First, consider if it's possible that this thought isn't true. I mean, based on what you've learned in this book so far, you know that the mind has an uncanny ability to make up stories with little regard for the facts, that it is lazy when it comes to finding difficult solutions, and that it's desperate to be right at the expense of the facts or other opinions (confirmation bias), especially when it is using judgment to build an identity, or to sustain the idea of self.

When considering all of this, our judgments feel less solid, and we are open to the idea that things are exactly as they should be, something that the mystics of all the world's great spiritual traditions have been saying for eons. In my work as a neuroscientist, I see this as a very right-brained way to see the world.

Another way to help question the validity of a thought is to talk it out with someone else. Candid alternate perspectives from someone you trust can be your ruler and will help you challenge irrational beliefs. Remember, your thoughts may still feel true. That's okay. Now you have some evidence that allows you to question what's really going on. Don't believe everything you think.

Most people have invasive thoughts, scary thoughts, and unwanted thoughts. If we think these thoughts define us in some way, or are true, they can become very disturbing and preoccupying. Phobias work this way too and can escalate into truly debilitating territory. I recall the case of a man who became desperately afraid he might hurt someone he loved with a knife. This was a kind man, who had many loving relationships and no history of violence or aggression. As part of his therapy, a psychologist decided to expose him to his fear by sitting in a room with him and a knife. This was of course terrifying for the man. But it immediately highlighted the difference between his invasive thoughts and his physical reality. Through safe exposure in a clinical setting, his body and mind could practice building comfort with the idea that his extreme thoughts and fears had nothing to do with an actual knife or an actual desire to harm anyone.

Practice: Find a Power Object

Many shamanic and spiritual practices incorporate the use of a power object. This can be a stone, a small figurine in the shape of an animal, a shell, or anything you feel drawn to. I like to work with something small enough to slip into my pocket so that when I find myself lost in the world of thinking, I can reach for and hold this object and remember that the mystery of its existence, and the mystery of my existence, are things that the thinking mind cannot think about. By its very existence, the power object reminds me not to believe everything I think.

Exercise: In Which Category Do the Squares Belong?

Cognitive scientists have had a difficult time explaining exactly how the mind forms its mental categories. Yes, you can think of a particular dog, but can you think of all possible examples that would fit into this category? If not, how do you know what your category is at all? Would a wolf fit into this category? Not really, but if we zoom out to the category of "canid," then we can include the wolf.

Categories can be changeable and hard to pin down even in the simplest cases. Things like white and black, or hot and cold, should be straightforward, right? Take a look at this visual illusion.

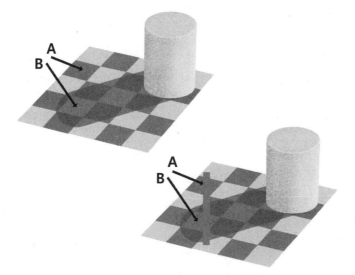

Which square would you put into the category of black? The A or B square?

Which square would you put into the category of white? The A or B square?

Would it surprise your mind to know that both squares are the same color and shade? The mind uses all sorts of guesses and assumptions (more abstractions) when it comes to creating its mental boxes. Sometimes, as in this case, the rules bend under certain conditions. One of the first psychologists, Hermann von Helmholtz, called this process unconscious inference.

Both A and B are, in reality, reflecting the same amount of light. That is, they are both the exact same shade of gray. However, the mind assumes that B is in the shade. Therefore, the only way it could give off the same amount of light as A, while it is in the shade, is if it was actually brighter than A. The mind makes this same assumption for A. If A is in the sun, the only way it could be the same level of energy as B, while it is in the sun, is if it was actually darker than B. These assumptions and guessing guide the mind to put A and B in different boxes, even if they are exactly the same in reality.

Practice: The Mind, Categories, and Physical Perception

Here is an even simpler experiment that requires just three bowls of water. In the middle, put a bowl of warm water. On the right, hot water (not burning hot, please); on the left, cold water. Put your right hand in the hot water and your left hand in the cold water for about thirty seconds. Then put both hands into the middle warm bowl. It's an interesting sensation. Both hands are in the same bowl, and both are feeling the same temperature. Yet to the right hand the water will feel cold, and to the left hand it will feel hot. Your brain knows for sure that the water in the bowl can only be one temperature, and yet each hand perceives it differently, because each has a different story connected to it.

Thinking about Thinking

Is the thinking mind ever able to think accurately about itself? Put another way, will the thinking mind ever understand how it functions? If it could, wouldn't it have already? As the old Zen saying goes, the eye cannot see itself. Might that apply to the mind too, stuck in its own illusion of self?

We've done exercises to expose the limitations of the thinking mind, and in most cases these were not discovered by people sitting down and thinking. They were discovered in research labs through physical and sensory experience, and the results were a total shock to the thinking minds involved in the experiment. Even with proof, most thinking minds still cannot accept the results of these research findings about the mind. My hope is that there is a part of you that realizes the limitations of the thinking mind and begins to put less faith in it as a result. This is what I call losing your mind.

If we can't convince our thinking minds to change even when we know the truth when it comes to low stakes riddles and lab experiments, is there any hope for clear consciousness or deeper enlightenment? Can we try to convince our thinking mind that it is not our self and unlock our suffering? Maybe not. After all, the thinking mind has served our species successfully (in its own way) for tens of thousands of years. However, we *can* begin to develop tools like the ones that expose visual illusions, like the ruler that demonstrates that two lines are indeed the same size. When it comes to practicing clear consciousness, these tools include discernment, presence, awareness, detachment or de-identifying, and quiet concentration. We might not be able to change our mind, but we can lose it and find some breath, some distance, and some joy. The thinking mind blocks us from knowing our true existence, but that doesn't mean we have to believe its chatter or accept its conclusions without question.

Thinking is truly an amazing trick that few ever think about, and while it has led to some extraordinary accomplishments in the real world, it has also led to intense mental suffering. This is largely because we live in a world that consists of only *thoughts* of the real world.

Falling Out of Love with Abstraction

The mind loves the abstract in the same way that banks love money: because without it, they can't exist. For instance, "cash" is just ink and wood; and most money these days isn't even that—it's ones and zeroes on a computer screen. Yet these abstractions have real, material consequences. Some of us are rich and others are poor. We feel elation or horror with the fluctuations of these numbers on the screen. Some people jump off buildings when the numbers go down. Whole mental outlooks, social theories, and systems of government are crafted around this abstraction. We might use this abstraction called money to alleviate real suffering in the world by meeting the basic needs of the estimated 2.8 billion people globally who live in poverty. But there are also many people who have plenty of money to meet their basic needs, and much more, and yet the abstraction of money accounts for a huge portion of their suffering and influences their beliefs and actions to an incredible degree.

Living in modern society means living in a world of abstractions that the mind created and thinks that it enjoys. You can also think of an abstraction as a simulation or fake, and the mind enjoys fakes because it has created them and finds them easier to process and less taxing to experience. Remember, abstraction is a way to detach from the real world, and that's what the mind does. This isn't a problem in and of itself; the thinking mind is simply doing what it is programmed to do. The problem comes when we mistake the mind's illusions for reality.

We're so in love with abstraction that modern society doesn't question for a moment having fake flowers in our homes, fake grass on our lawns, or even fake friends and followers floating in the extreme abstraction of social media. If an alien dropped down to earth, how would you explain these things? These fakes are so far detached from reality as to be comical.

Another way to think of the mind's love for abstraction is as a virus, spreading to new tissue and new hosts. Symptoms include nonstop thinking about the past, the future, and abstractions standing in for places, objects, relationships, and more. The mind carries the past around like an old pair of glasses, seeing the present through the lens of what we think happened before. Yet the past is just another abstract world in which many of us choose to live. Dragging the past into the present blunts the jagged newness of the now. If we put our experiences into the box of "Monday" or "winter" or "lunch," we feel we can manage them by making them ordinary, known, or predictable. But there are no ordinary moments.

Most people are under the illusion that they have a single job that they do every week. Whether they are a nurse, driver, CEO, cook, writer, etc., this idea of a single job is an illusion. You never do the same job twice—ever. You don't even live through the same moment twice! Yet every time you go to work, your mind gets busy finding similarities and making connections (memory and categorization) so that you feel like it's a dreaded Monday and another week of the same old thing.

In reality, everything is different, every time. Change is the only constant. This was one of the fundamental insights of the Buddha—that physical reality is continuously in a state of change. Even if you have filled out the same report a dozen times, this time is different. The mind's tendency to create a stable, unchanging self is the same tendency that makes it feel like you do the same job every day.

In many wisdom practices, one is reminded to have the mind of a beginner or a child. This is because for a beginner or a child, everything is new and exciting. There are no expectations because there have been no categories formed. Approaching the present from this place of openness and curiosity is one way to fall out of love with the thinking mind's abstractions and fall in love with the mystery of clear consciousness.

Falling in Love with the Present Moment

Are you in the present moment? Does the moment feel fresh, as it is, or are you looking at it through the lens of the past? The ancient Greek philosopher Heraclitus said, "You cannot step into the same river twice." Of course, one of the main teachings of Buddhism is that everything is changing all the time, and anything believed to be consistent and stable is an illusion. Each moment happens only once. Each moment is as unique and individual as any creation in the universe. The belief that any moment is the same as any past moment is just the mind bringing the past along for the ride. The mind is categorizing.

Buddhism provides many avenues that return us to the present moment and our experience of it. In fact, the present is the only time that we have access to, ever.

Practice: It Is Still Now

I always enjoy using language to point to the now. This mini practice can be done anytime simply by repeating this short mantra:

It is now. It is still now. It is still now.

You can say it a few times, or until you start to feel your thinking mind detach from its own words and really feel the truth of the statement. It is always now. Always the present moment.

Try doing this . . . now.

Practice: Learn from Nonhumans

While many animals have habits of mind that create illusions and abstractions, nonhuman beings often manage to stay more connected to the present moment. Become an observer of a nonhuman being. Remember that even if your mind wants to put them into a category (dog, tree, bird . . .), each being is unique in the world exactly as it is. The mind can have its folly, don't worry. In the meantime, use these questions as a jumping-off point to be more curious and present in the moment.

- The mind has placed this being into so many mental categories. What are ten ways that this being exists beyond any of those mental boxes?

- What happens when I sync up my breathing with the breathing of this being? What if I put my body in the same position, or look in the same direction, or sniff the same thing?

Allow this nonhuman being to be your guide to the present moment in a new way.

Everything about this moment is unique and original and will never happen again. It is time to come home, back to the real world. The mind will continue with its thought-driven fantasies, but we know these are all variations on a theme.

The Mind Is a Problem Creator, Not a Problem Solver

Our mind thinks that mental boxes will solve our problems, but more often our mental boxes make our problems grow. I would bet that your everyday life includes access to clean running water, as well as a stove, microwave, refrigerator, washer and dryer, dishwasher, and vacuum cleaner. Your food comes mostly from a grocery store or restaurant (even if you live on a farm). You drive a car, ride a bicycle, or take public transportation to get that food a good portion of the time.

Just a short time ago, gathering, transporting, storing, and preparing basics such as food and water required many hours of work. Most of that work has now been eliminated by technology, yet I bet your left brain has complained recently about your car, the need to go to the store, the time it takes to get someplace, or some task related to any of the other miraculous time-saving inventions I mentioned. This isn't a guilt trip about how good you have it, but rather a lesson to demonstrate the true source of "problems" in your life. First-world problems are all due to the mind—that's it. With more stability comes more technology, and the mind has less and less to do, so it must expand the mental box of "What is a problem?" The mind is just doing what it's good at!

Many reading this will remember the 1990s sitcom *Seinfeld*. The show explored aspects of the mind in funny and creative ways and was the most popular show at the time. In one episode, one of the characters buys a beautiful white cashmere sweater for a friend at a deeply discounted price due to a small, almost imperceptible red dot. One by one, each character gets taken in by the beauty of the sweater only to discover the dot, which makes the sweater unacceptable. When each discovers the spot, they quickly want to get rid of the sweater and pass it on to the next character.

This episode illustrates how a problem is created by the mind instead of solved by it. The beautiful, warm sweater did its job, but an almost imperceptible blemish made every character's mind imagine it was "bad" or "wrong." This comical setup points to the very nature of the problem with our problems.

In the same way that a doctor may believe that a drug isn't working so they crank up the dose, the mind believes that more mind is the answer to the problem of mind. *Of course, the only problem with this is that the thinking mind is the problem.*

The very real survival challenges that the human mind evolved to address have largely disappeared, but the mind keeps busily expanding the category of "problem" in order to find a problem to solve, even if there is nothing wrong. In a well-protected, secure home, with access to water and food, the mind has very little to do, so it invents problems that are simply not real.

I'm not suggesting that we live in a world without real problems. Poverty, disease, and many other serious, complicated problems require real solutions. If you are in physical pain or don't have enough money for food or shelter, then a large portion of your thinking mind's energy is no doubt dealing with these real issues. (Yet it's likely also inventing all sorts of sideshow problems at the same time, pulling energy away from much needed solutions.) Furthermore, even though many modern problems are abstractions, they still cause real suffering that can be felt in the body, mind, and soul. Anyone who has had a panic attack knows that thoughts, while abstractions, have real-world effects.

Many of our problems result from an overactive mind, one where the left side of the brain is constantly perceiving and categorizing things into buckets of "good" and "bad," "desirable" and "dangerous." Because of this, the thinking mind will constantly seek out ways to make comparisons (the building block of categorization), and find problems as a result. Again, let's resist the urge to label this process "bad" in a left-brain way. This is just what the left brain does, which is only a problem when we are so identified with the left brain that we think it's us. Then the problems the mind creates become "our problems," and a whole world of suffering and avoidance comes into being.

Exercise: First-World Problems

Ask yourself, *What is wrong with my life right now?*

See if you can decide which of these problems is the silliest. If you're stuck, a quick search of videos on YouTube with the phrase "first-world problems" will bring up some outrageous ones.

Here's one to get you started: I have a friend whose mother-in-law planned a fancy holiday brunch at a restaurant, and she was incensed that the management didn't feel comfortable asking their servers to wear the flamingo-themed aprons that the hostess had purchased and provided for the event. It was a *real problem* to her in the moment.

Here are some more examples: The air-conditioning is too cold right now. My new shoes are too tight and are not worn in yet. My sports car doesn't shift between gears as smoothly as I would like. My cell phone audio quality isn't as good as my friends'. Last night's pizza was delivered late and wasn't as hot as I wanted. Write down your own, and then take a look at the following questions:

- Is it really you making these silly complaints?

- Isn't there a part of you that knows these problems are silly? Almost laughable?

- Where does that feeling coming from?

- How could the part that is laughing come from the same place that is creating the problem?

Imagine if you could go back in time and return with a visitor from three hundred years ago. How would you explain your silly problems to this person? How would you feel making such complaints to them? Really go into this. Imagine explaining to someone why it is such a disappointment that your cell phone gets poor reception, or that your dinner order was twenty minutes late and not as hot as you desired.

Doesn't it seem like the thinking mind is kind of ridiculous and out of touch? It is.

Problem Inflation

A recent study sheds light on why, for many of us, even a small issue like a red dot on a fancy sweater (or any other silly problem) can be viewed as a serious issue. One group of subjects was asked to detect a blue dot among a series of images flashed in front of them. Another group of subjects had to detect a threatening face. And a final group of subjects had to detect if a proposed research project was ethical. This all seems very straightforward, and in a logical world not dominated by the biased program of the mind, such decisions would be easy to make.

The trick is that the researchers gradually slowed down the appearance of each of the various targets as the experiment progressed. Blue dots, threatening faces, and unethical proposals showed up less and less until they disappeared altogether. Did subjects simply stop seeing blue dots, threatening faces, and unethical proposals? *No, they changed how they defined the target.*

As blue dots appeared less and less, subjects started to see purple dots and believe they were blue. As threatening faces appeared less and less, subjects started to perceive nonthreatening faces as threatening. And as unethical research papers became fewer and fewer, subjects redefined what was and wasn't ethical so they could still find more "unethical papers." Quite fascinatingly, as the real targets (or problems) disappeared, the minds involved inflated the category to make sure there was still a problem to solve.[25]

What's more, the effect described above took place *even when the subjects were told to expect this*! Yet again, we find that one cannot stop inventing problems by intellectually knowing how the mind works. The only way we can hope to get out of this thinking problem is to put some space between the true us and the thinking mind.

Practice: Revisit Your "Problems"

The next time you find yourself fixated on a problem, recognize that it is not you that is making this judgment but rather the mind that has focused on this one imperfection and then let that ruin the entire event. Remember, the left brain's narrow focus will shine a spotlight on the flaws and lose sight of the big picture, which is inevitably filled with miracles and abundance.

- Is the problem you think you have a matter of attention?

- Are you focusing on only a small part of reality and calling it a problem and at the same time missing out on everything that is perfect as it is?

Refocus. Change your attention to the positive aspects of the situation. Remember that attention is a strange thing. Like breathing, it will carry on running its program without your input. But you can also bring a certain amount of clear, conscious control to what's happening in the thinking mind. See something else that you are thankful for. Tell the story in a different way.

Practice: Stop Seeking

I would guess that anyone reading this book lives better than a king. What I mean is, you and I eat better food, enjoy better health, and are probably more comfortable than the average medieval king or queen. For most of our lives, we don't really need anything more than what we have easy access to. We may not need it, that is, but *oh boy do we want it*.

The whole field of marketing is built on the foundation of the left brain's compulsion to always be in need of something new, something else, something better. Our focus on first-world problems will continue to make us feel like we don't have enough. This is a scarcity mindset, a story that's particularly addictive to the mind, which evolved to pay close attention to not having enough food and supplies. Even when we do have enough, scarcity keeps us on a hamster wheel of wanting more, more, more. It keeps us believing that whatever we have right now is not enough. Modern marketing has discovered an even more insidious kind of scarcity, not just of possessions but also a scarcity of inner worth. If we believe that *who we are* is not enough, that our personal flaws can be fixed with more of this or that, then our desire to seek solutions will never be quenched. This is the secret sauce of marketing.

Coco Chanel said, "Elegance is refusal." One path to contentment is to refuse the mind's habit of always seeking things. Make it a practice to refuse. When your mind reacts to a message that you "need something" or you're not enough, simply thank your mind for its input and say, *No, thank you. I have enough of everything in the present moment.* Remember at the beginning of this book, when we talked about starting small. This is a perfect practice to try out in a tiny way. Stop seeking something you think you need, and see what happens.

Gratitude

In my mindfulness class, we cover the practice of gratitude and how being thankful for what we have can rewire the brain in a very short time. When the problem solving (and also problem creating) mind is recognized for what it is, one instantly welcomes in and makes space for the sensation of gratitude. Because it is the thinking mind that feels regret, lack, revenge, and the negative emotions we evolved for survival, once you realize this isn't who you are, you minimize the powerful hold of these emotions.

Gratitude practices often take the form of making lists of things we feel grateful for. This approach of counting our blessings employs the thinking mind's categorization system against itself. It's a way of consciously shifting the boxes in a way that more accurately reflects our current reality. It reminds us that we tend to take many good things for granted. If you haven't tried this, you can build a daily or weekly practice of writing down a few things for which you're grateful every day.

As a variation, you may do what one friend of mine does and put those gratitude items on small slips of paper and drop them into a big jar. Then, as a new year's tradition, she takes them all out and reads them, sometimes even putting them in categories to see what themes emerge over time. In this way, gratitude can fuel a process of authentic goal setting, aligning with what we really value and working to bring more of it into our lives.

Interestingly, recent research has highlighted that there is an even more powerful gratitude practice than this daily download of blessings. In his Huberman Lab podcast, Andrew Huberman, a professor of neurobiology and ophthalmology at Stanford, synthesizes these findings and suggests the following gratitude protocol that can increase our overall health and well-being.[26]

Practice: Telling a Story of Gratitude

This is a practice to do around three times per week, or more if you find it helpful. Start by thinking of or remembering a time when you received genuine, heartfelt gratitude from another person or creature. Maybe it was a letter from a former student, or a time when you were genuinely thanked for going out of your way to make someone else's life better. Alternatively, this could be a time when you observed someone else giving and/or receiving wholehearted gratitude. The more you can feel the emotional power of this memory or story, the better.

Using a narrative, or story, about gratitude for this practice—whether or not you experienced it personally or simply observed, read, or heard about it—draws on the storytelling and story-believing strengths of the thinking mind.

You will use the same story every time you do the exercise, so take a little time to jot down three or four quick reminders about the story to cue your memory of it. These should include the situation before the gratitude was expressed, how it felt afterward, and why the story had emotional weight.

The practice itself is short. Review your three or four reminders, and then spend one or two minutes feeling into the genuine experience of that expression of gratitude. Notice if it brings up any physical sensations, and gently allow any emotions to wash over you.

Just as the ancient Buddhist notion of no self is being substantiated by modern research, cognitive science is also catching up with what wisdom teachers have known for millennia about the power of gratitude to deepen our connection to our true self.

Practice: The Simplest Path to Gratitude

If you find it difficult to bring gratitude into the picture because of the negative clouds of the thinking mind, you might try simply focusing on the fact that right now you are a conscious being. Perhaps you have no money in the bank or are dealing with an uncertain future in terms of your health. Nonetheless, right now, you are aware and conscious. This is the greatest gift possible.

For years, I've put this question to my students: "If you could be rich, famous, and powerful but not conscious, would you take the deal?" To date, not a single person would take it. Perhaps your consciousness is aware of the sun on your face, or a slight wind blowing, or the faint scent of flowers. The greatest gift of gratitude is always right in front of us because it *is* us. It is our consciousness.

I'm willing to bet that there's nothing in this material world that you would trade for your precious consciousness. Remembering this is the simplest path to gratitude.

Letting Go of the Past

We've seen how the mind creates problems by stirring up our fears and amplifying issues. The thinking mind also affects our ability to forgive others and even our ability to forgive ourselves. It seems normal and natural to judge ourselves and others, hold a grudge, or punish ourselves or others for perceived wrongs. And yet, based on what you know now about the thinking mind and the fictitious self it creates, is it possible that these certainties might not hold up, just like those visual illusions fall apart when faced with a ruler? How can we judge another for a self that was nothing but a flickering light (a self) that went out long ago, that is never the same moment to moment? Of course, this also holds when we can't forgive ourselves, because we are attached to a version of a past "self" that a current self cannot accept. The cognitive dissonance is too painful.

In many ways a resentment, a grudge, or an inability to extend forgiveness results from a bundle of thoughts that have been placed in a mental box and put on life support by the mind.

Practice: Forgiveness

Some "imperfections" are part of a thing: a dent on a new car, a flaw in a diamond, a red dot on a cashmere sweater. Other "imperfections" are actions that are then remembered by the mind: someone did something a long time ago, or you did something a long time ago. One path to forgiveness is to bring awareness to the mind's creation of categories and mental boxes, and expand your focus beyond these categories. You might even envision a little animation in your head in which your thinking mind has placed some old event into a mental box and marked it "unforgivable." Yes, that probably sounds strange, but in a way this is what has happened.

For this exercise, consider a situation from the past that your mind is having a difficult time letting go of. Perhaps it is an issue that you feel is unforgivable or that brings up feelings of regret or even shame. Ponder the following questions:

- Does this event exist when I'm not thinking about it?

- Do I keep this issue alive by thinking about it?

- Does ruminating on this problem draw away energy and awareness from the present moment?

- Am I missing out on knowing what is, or the chance to see and repair relationships in the present (with myself or others), because of the weight of what's in this box?

If a person acted like a jerk ten years ago, that jerk could be long gone. The interaction now exists only in our minds as a memory. When we judge someone on the past, we are putting them in the same mental box as today's reality, bringing back to life a situation that existed a long time ago. I'm sure you are a different person now—and likely, so are they.

Practice: Repairing Harm

Just as the suffering of poverty is very real, the tendency of the mind to hold on to wrongs in abstract mental boxes does not negate real harm. However, very often when we create these abstractions of "bad" or "unforgiveable" behavior, it has the ironic and unfortunate result of cutting off our access to repairing the harm. The abstractions block real healing because the abstractions are not real.

The Japanese practice of *kintsukuroi* is an art of repairing broken objects by focusing on the "flaws" created by the harm and turning them into a central positive feature of a renewed object. Practitioners of this ancient art would fix broken pottery by using tree sap dusted with gold to glue the pieces back together. In the end, the repaired piece was considered far superior. This art challenges the mind's rigidity when it comes to categorizing something as "bad" forever.

Often in life, things the mind views as negative or flawed can turn out to be one of the best parts of our existence, something we would never change even if we could. Examples include a divorce, loss of a job, being alone, failure, or any other "broken" part of our lives.

Practice: Kintsukuroi on Your Memories

Find something in your past that at the time you were convinced was "horrible." Think of the days, weeks, and years that followed this event or time in your life. What kind of metaphorical tree sap did you use to glue things back together? What gold dust made the brokenness whole again, and more beautiful than before? Would you change things if you could? Even if the answer is yes, there are no doubt many ways in which your current experience is beautiful in its brokenness and in its wholeness. That is part of what it means to be human.

Was there any way in which that past "terrible" thing made your life more meaningful? Do you have gratitude for this event and/or its aftermath?

It's easier to perform kintsukuroi on events from the past, from your current perspective. The next thing I'm going to ask you to try is a bit more difficult.

Can you find something in your life *right now* to which you can apply this kind of tender repair? Is there something happening for you right now that you have categorized as "bad" but perhaps you are wrong? Can you think of three ways to be grateful for it right now?

How does this change the experience of thinking about this event in your mind? Can you put a little space in between the feelings that come up and your sense of self? Can you entertain the idea that your relationship to this event will continue to change as you stay in the present moment, and not the past or the future?

Remember, we use categorization to see our endlessly changing reality as a false consistency. One of the main insights of the Buddha was to recognize that reality was continuously changing and that our suffering was the result of clinging to our idea that it is somewhat stable and consistent, like the idea of a "me" or a "self."

Memory as the Tool of the Self

How does your personality come into being? By memory. By identifying the present with the past and projecting it into the future. Think of yourself as momentary, without past and future, and your personality dissolves.
—Sri Nisargadatta Maharaj

All animals and insects (and probably some fungi, plants, and bacteria as well) learn from the past. It's difficult to imagine how any species could survive or evolve without at least a rudimentary, nonthinking ability to remember. While the benefits of memory are clear, in this section we will see how memories create and support our illusion of a self in ways that amp up our suffering.

Much of what neuroscience has learned about the memory-making process comes from studying individuals with damage to certain areas of their brains. For example, there have been significant cases in which brain areas were damaged or removed, resulting in an almost total loss of the ability to form new memories.

One of the most notable individuals in this regard was Henry Molaison, or H. M., as he is better known in textbooks.[27] Henry suffered from a brain disease requiring experimental surgery that removed a part of the brain that we now know is critical to forming new memories—the temporal lobe. The surgery took place in 1953, when he was twenty-seven years old, and afterward he was unable to form any new memories.

In 2007, for Henry, nothing new had happened since 1953. Truman was still president and he still believed he was in his late twenties. As he grew older, his ongoing belief that he was in his twenties resulted in a profound sense of shock upon seeing his aged reflection in the mirror.

Henry passed in 2008, and living for fifty-five years without new memories puts in stark relief something that all of us take for granted: We know what happened a few moments ago, and a few moments before that. In a famous quote describing his own experience, Henry stated, "Right now, I'm wondering. Have I done or said anything amiss? You see, at this moment everything looks clear to me, but what happened just before? That's what worries me. It's like waking from a dream; I just don't remember."[28]

For Henry, even a minor distraction would result in him forgetting what he was discussing. After age twenty-seven, he would meet the same people, including neighbors when he was out for walks, or researchers and doctors who were trying to help him, and each time it was as if he was meeting them for the first time.

Almost.

You see, Henry's wife recounted that when re-meeting those with whom he had had positive experiences in prior encounters, Henry would seem to warm up more quickly. Yes, he would still have to go through the process of introduction each time, but his prior experience with a person seemed to have some carryover effect on the tenor of the interaction, at least in some cases.

Furthermore, the late researcher and neuroscientist Suzanne Corkin, who worked with Henry for forty-three years, explains that he could retain some new motor skills such as learning how to ride a bike, playing tennis, or even learning to play the piano. These activities fall under what some in the field of neuroscience call "unconscious memory."

The term *unconscious* is something that science applies to a wide range of things that occur in the body that the mind isn't actively thinking about, such as the digestive system, the nervous system, etc. In my view, this definition of *unconscious* really means "things the left-brain interpreter doesn't have regular access to." The brain and nervous system are no doubt directing these processes, so it doesn't make sense to separate them out or minimize them in relation to the activities of the thinking mind.

When Henry died at the age of eighty-two, he had no egoic collection of personal memories from his final five decades. For most of us, these are the kinds of memories that define who we are. To an outsider looking in, Henry's story had a huge piece missing. This begs the question, If we use our memories to define ourselves, what does that mean for people like Henry? Did Henry need the story of a self beyond twenty-seven to be happy? In an interview near the end of Henry's life, he was asked if his life was happy even without these autobiographical memories of a self and his response was yes.

One of the lessons we can glean from Henry is that being attached to our personal story based on autobiographical memories doesn't make us happy. In fact, I believe the less we are attached to it, the happier we can be. So, while what happened to Henry was tragic and we wouldn't wish it upon anyone, perhaps the lesson is that it's good to have the memories, but we don't have to identify with them so much or look to them for happiness. Our memories don't have to control us.

Now let's contrast the case of H. M. with that of Solomon Shereshevsky, or S, as he is known in textbooks. S was a man who remembered too much; a Russian who was studied extensively by Alexander Luria, who many refer to as the father of modern neuropsychology. According to Luria, S was gifted with a near photographic memory, and able to recall exact conversations and events that had taken place years ago.

In fact, he could remember so many details that he wanted to forget them, and in most cases he could not. His unbelievable memory, in this way, seemed to S to feel more like a heavy burden than a gift. Luria recounts how S had trouble completing tasks and focusing in the present because something would always remind him of a past event, and it was as if his incredible memory kept him trapped in the past. Furthermore, S had very little ability to understand metaphor; everything was literal for him.[29] Interestingly, the left side of the brain is involved with literal understanding and the right brain finds meaning in the big picture—a key feature of metaphor.

One thing is for sure: memory is key for the creation of the self. Even in Henry's case, the self he created prior to age twenty-seven was the same one he woke up with every morning, and he was shocked every time he looked in the mirror and saw an old man he didn't recognize.

Exercise: Faulty Memory

Another thing that cognitive science has shown us is that our memory is not as good as we think it is. Let's take a look at the following exercise.

First, read the following list of ten words and then cover them up and keep reading.

- Dream

- Night

- Dusk

- Snooze

- Dark

- Snore

- Alarm

- Covers

- Bed

- Sheets[30]

Are they covered up? Okay, now the rest is simple: Were any of the following words on the list?

- Aardvark

- Intelligence

- Sleep

If you are like the vast majority of my students, I get a loud, confident "Yes!" to "Sleep." But if you check the list, you won't find it there. The interpretive mind created a memory of what likely happened, not what actually happened. Our memories are not videotapes of the past but more like a highly distorted, biased image of what we *think* happened. Furthermore, our memories have been demonstrated to change and shift dramatically over time. The truth is that memories are really just more thoughts.

Memories Are Myths

Think about one of your favorite days. Now think of one of your not so favorite days. What did you have for breakfast this morning? How did you celebrate your last birthday? Each of these memories is a kind of myth. At most, it is a story made up of thoughts, and you have no access to it from the reality of the present moment, except as a pure abstraction.

Yet we are so attached to our memories that we allow them to dictate how we approach the present moment. We would rather guess about this moment based on distortions from our past than expose ourselves to the great unknown of being where we are right now. How will you know if today is a good day unless you can compare it to the mind's image of the past? A day at the park could be like a fantasy to someone who has memories of years in prison, but to a world-traveling adventurer with different memories it could be boring, even confining.

When we recall a memory, words and pictures just pop from mind into awareness. They convince us that things happened the way we think they happened. Most of us are aware on some level that the memories we have of events in our lives don't always reflect what really happened; but when we dig deeper, we discover that the process is even more profound. Your memory is only a story of a story of a story. *In fact, none of your memories ever happened.* The mind only stores what it *thinks* happened. Remember the definition of cognition? We only store a highly modified and distorted version of reality—not reality.

Memory is a myth because memories are just like any other thoughts: they are products of the mind. Since the 1950s, neuroscientists have tried to find where memory lives in the brain, and they have come up short every time. In the same way that neuroscientists cannot find thoughts in the brain, they cannot find memories either. Thoughts are not at all what they seem to be, and it turns out that memories aren't, either.

In the '80s, William F. Brewer and James C. Treyens did one of the first studies to show that our memories are only what we *think* happened.[31] They had subjects wait in a professor's office for thirty-five seconds and then, after leaving, they had to recall all the objects in the office. Rather than simply recalling what was in the office, they recalled what they thought would be in a professor's office. For example, in this office Brewer and Treyens made sure there were no books; but almost a third of the subjects "remembered" that there were books in the office. They remembered what they thought happened, not what actually happened.

The myth of memory accuracy has a history of profound effects in the courtroom. The psychologist Elizabeth Loftus investigated the memory process in the courtroom only to find it often resulted in devastating, life-changing consequences. It has been estimated that 70 percent of wrongful convictions are due to incorrect eyewitness identification.

In one case, a man was suspected of a terrible crime—burglary and rape. The victim picked this individual out of a police lineup and stated with complete confidence that he was the one who'd done it. He was convicted and spent ten years in prison before DNA evidence and a confession from another man proved his innocence. After finding the actual criminal, it was clear that this wasn't a case of two people looking alike. In fact, the two didn't resemble each other at all.[32]

The first problem is that no eyewitness can replay a precise recording of what they saw; they can only recall what they *think* happened. The second, perhaps more serious, problem is that most eyewitnesses do not know the first problem exists. We tend to trust our own memories, and we trust them even more when those memories connect to a rare, dangerous, or high-impact moment, like witnessing or being the victim of a crime. It rarely occurs to us that everything we ever "remember" includes projections from our thinking mind. These projections will largely depend on our past experiences, compounded by problematic filters such as structural racism and sexism.

Most remarkably in this case is that even after spending ten years in prison for a crime he didn't commit, the innocent man was able to forgive the victim whose testimony sent him to prison. While we don't know his personal path to forgiveness, I believe that when one recognizes the processes of the mind, one is capable of any act of forgiveness. Not just forgiveness of others but also of oneself.

Here's the thing: Memory forms one of the most fundamental aspects of the creation of the fictitious self. Memory allows us to create a chain of events in our mind that are central to establishing the idea that "all of this happened to me." We can then replay these memories over and over and apply them to any situation. This serves us well in many ways — our existence would be unrecognizable without memory — but it also comes with some problematic consequences. Much of our suffering arises from replaying memories and projecting them onto what we think might happen in the future. This is the very definition of regret and anxiety.

One way to alleviate the suffering tied to our memories is to consciously work to loosen our sense of identification between our memories and our fictitious sense of self.

Practice: Less Certainty about Your Memories

When you recognize that memories are not facts but interpretations made by the brain, you may find yourself shifting from "this is what happened" to "this is what I think happened" or "this is the story I am telling myself about what happened." This simple shift can become a profound practice.

You can try doing this in ways with low stakes. Remember a recent interaction and tell the story of what happened with as much detail and accuracy as you can muster but add the words "I think" before each "factual" statement. See how this feels in your body. Does it make you uncertain? Uncomfortable? Does it increase your curiosity or just annoy you? Perhaps you don't have to be "right" about what you remember to reap the learning and predicting benefits of memory. Maybe you can hold your memories with a little less reverence.

You can also try retelling the story of one of your most certain memories—something you know in your gut that is "real." Relate it to yourself again, talking out loud or writing it down, and insert a little bit of healthy skepticism with words and phrases like "maybe," "it's possible that," "I think," or "from my current vantage point."

Over time, you might notice that your relations with others, even strangers, become lighter and less serious when you are not so certain of exactly what happened.

Memories and Self

I have said that scientists have not been able to locate thoughts and memories in the brain. But they have discovered that different types of memories are processed in different areas in the brain. For example, if you play a musical instrument or a certain sport for years, at some point you just know how to do it and you can perform without thinking. Clive Wearing, a patient with a case similar to H. M., couldn't remember anything that happened more than seven seconds prior; but he still remembered how to play the piano like a concert pianist.

Information about the self and memories that make up the sense of self fire up in different areas of the brain than these long-term skill memories. Memories that form the story of you almost always correlate to a time and place: "Where did I leave my keys yesterday?" "Where did I park my car today?" "What food did I like best as a child?"

The idea of a self depends on these types of memories, called autobiographical memories. They are about your story. When someone asks, "Who are you?" the first thing we do is rely on these special types of thoughts. We call up all kinds of categories that make up "us." I am my name, my gender, my job, my age, my personality. These are all thoughts of what we think happened in the past and they define what we think of as a stable sense of identity of self. This can be as basic as memories about your attributes and as complex as secrets from your past that inform your behavior in subtle ways. For example, if I say, "I'm an introvert," it is because I am thinking of events that happened in the past. Perhaps I remember that I was at several social events in which I felt uncomfortable and just wanted to be alone.

Finish this statement in any possible way and it will almost certainly depend on some type of memory:

I am _____.

Memories Are Reconstructions

Whenever we recall a memory, we reconstruct it. When we remember or recollect, we are putting together a story of what we think happened, not witnessing or replaying what happened. So, none of our memories ever really happened in the first place. I repeat: *None of my memories ever happened the way I think they did.* Because perceptions and beliefs are products of the left brain, then our memories are our biased interpretations of the past and therefore illusions or dreams at best.

How can we use this knowledge to decrease the suffering caused by memories and harness the power of the storytelling mind to bring us into clear consciousness?

What if we began to think of memories less as reconstructions of reality and more as collages of different pieces, times, and versions that don't have to be brought together into a single coherent truth? What if we allowed memories to be embellishments or interpretations of the past? Simply knowing that your memories aren't cold, hard facts can change how we relate to others and lessen the suffering in our minds.

Exercise: Being Henry

What if we lost our story? What if we lost the memories that are used to construct the self? As a thought experiment, let's go back to the earlier "I am _____." But rather than filling it in with anything that relies on a memory, only use what is happening right now, in the present moment. You can't use a name, because that is just a memory of what others call you. You can't use your job title, or anything that requires a memory. You are just like Henry; you have lost your story. Go.

I am _____.

Through this exercise, you may discover just how reliant you are on memories and expectations to frame your current experience. Go deeper. Rather than saying you are "chilly" because you are comparing the room temperature to many other past room temperatures, experiment with simply describing the physical sensation. Even if it doesn't make a lot of sense. "I am shivery shoulders." "I am this inhale." "I am this exhale." "I am a stream of disconnected thoughts." The only thing you are without memory is awareness itself. Clear consciousness.

This is a very practical way to come into the present moment and distance yourself from what psychologists call rumination, a thinking pattern that brings up old memories again and again and is a major factor in depression and anxiety. Consider that you can't take any thought or memory seriously or literally. The self-illusion depends on these types of thoughts as the illusory self persists in suffering. That is, it would rather reassert itself and exist, even if the price is suffering, than experience the unknown freedom of no self.

One other hint: The mind will also try to ignore these exercises by taking the argument to the extreme and saying something like, *You mean World War II never happened?* or *But I was in a car accident last year that totaled my car and put me in the hospital. Are you saying that never happened?* Without a doubt, the suffering of these events is genuine, even if the stories behind them, fueled by memories, are an illusion. Our memories are certainly good for some things— finding our lost car keys, steering clear of dangerous situations— but they can also lead us astray. In fact, we could say that much of the suffering in the world arises from the negative aspects of the thinking mind, which can easily inflate its will to survive into bigotry, hatred, and even violence.

The thinking mind obsesses over the past in the form of memories and rumination, and fixates on the future in the form of predictions, worries, and anxiety. One antidote to the worrying mind is to become a scientist and test its effectiveness. In short, you will run the following experiment to decide if the time and energy you spend on worrying yields a comparable positive mitigation of suffering. Is worrying a good use of your time?

Exercise: Your Worry List

Consider your current worries and write them all down in list form. Journal about your thoughts and what you think is going to happen, and then give each item a number that signifies how confident you are that your prediction will come true, with 1 being that you highly doubt your worry will come to pass, and 10 being near certain that your worry will play out in the way you think it will. Put this list away.

Come back to your list in a week to two to see how accurate your worries and predictions turned out to be. When I do this practice at the beginning of a semester with students, they find that fewer than half of their predictions ever turn out to be true. This doesn't seem like a very good return on investment of time and energy. Our future predictions and our memories are inaccurate most of the time. Despite this, most of us spend a lot of time thinking about the future and past. If we can see how unreliable our thoughts are in these areas, then we can release them and be in the now. We can say to our ruminating and predictive minds, *Thanks for your input, but I know that you're not usually right—so I'm going to recenter myself in what's happening right now.*

The Fiction of "Normal"

The left brain loves statistics. I'm not talking about the college class that everyone loathes; I mean the abstract concept of averages and normal. We talk about the average weather this month, the average wealth, average height, average weight, even the average number of years a person lives.

We describe groups by their averages or what we call a mean. Consider the following example of numbers: 2, 3, 4, 5, 6. It might be easy to see that the average is 4. Technically, you just add up all the numbers (20) and divide by how many numbers there are (5) to get 4. In both the sciences and in many everyday problems, we might use 4 to describe the whole group in the same way that the word *phone* is used to represent the thing in your pocket and the one on your desk. It's a shorthand way of describing them and, like other categorizations of the mind, it can be very useful as long as you know that you are not dealing with something real.

This isn't to say that averages are not useful abstractions. If you see that your average coffee consumption has gone down by a couple cups a day, that can be helpful if you're tracking how much caffeine you consume. If your blood pressure is 120 over 80, that's good to know it's in the normal range.

But what is lost on most of us is that the more abstract something is, the more it exists only as an idea in the mind and not in reality. Consider this example: In 3, 3, 5, 5, the mean is still 4. But 4 isn't a member of the group. It doesn't exist in the group even if it is representing it. In a sense, this is just like the mind-made self; it is an abstraction that doesn't exist. This can lead us into dangerous territory if we orient our reality to an average.

In his book *The End of Average: The Science of What Makes Us Different*, Todd Rose tells the incredible story of airplane engineering after World War II. In the 1940s, at the dawn of jet-powered aviation, the American Air Force found itself with a life-or-death problem. Its aircraft were crashing in noncombat accidents and incidents—up to seventeen in a single day. Pilots were retrained, trainers were retrained, tests were run and rerun confirming the mechanical functioning of the planes themselves. All to no avail. What could it be?

As it turns out, the original 1926 cockpit design was based on averages of the measurements of hundreds of pilots at the time. The Air Force updated these measurements in 1950 by measuring four thousand pilots from their thumb length to their head circumference and everything in between. They averaged all these measurements again and got similar numbers to 1926. Then, one scientist had a hunch and set out to investigate how many active-duty pilots' measurements actually matched the average. As it turns out, the answer was zero. The cockpit was designed for no one.

This discovery led to the realization that the crashes were due to a design problem, not pilot or mechanical error. Because these new jets were so much more complicated to fly, pilots had to be able to adjust their seats, and gain easy access to many more levers and buttons. Making the cockpit adjustable eliminated most accidents, improved performance, and increased the range of body types that could fly planes. As it turned out, planes designed for the individuals flying them worked better.[33]

This is important to remember when we're thinking in averages. They can be useful when they remain abstract, but they crumble as soon as we try to apply them to reality in any specific way. When we say someone is just a "normal person," we are speaking of a fiction upon a fiction. When we say that today is a "normal day," we are speaking from the perspective of the left brain's narrow spotlight focus, which cherry-picks aspects of today and matches them up with other days to create the category of "normal." No single day, person, or moment will ever be "normal." This is a gift.

Categorization

In a classic scene from the film *The Wizard of Oz*, Dorothy and her companions have returned to the throne room of the great wizard who they think can grant their various hearts' desires. The wizard dismisses them, until Dorothy's dog Toto draws everyone's attention to a small curtain near the back of the room. Toto pulls the curtain aside, revealing the "wizard" to be just a regular man, furiously turning dials and pushing buttons, and shouting into a microphone, "Pay no attention to the man behind the curtain!" Once the spectacle of the wizard is revealed for what it is, however, illusion falls away, and Dorothy's friends are all able to move forward with their true dreams and aspirations.

This is, of course, a wonderful metaphor for the left brain interpreter.

When we don't know the cause of a problem, it's very easy to keep spinning in circles. The left brain interpreter relies on this spinning for its very existence, so it spends much of its time pulling off an impressive magic trick. It convinces us that our thoughts are real by making it impossible, even for the mind itself, to *think* about the processes that create those thoughts in the first place. So, we believe our thoughts reflect the problems in our life, rather than recognizing that much of the time, our thoughts *are* the problem.

As a result, we work to solve this or that single problem but never get to the true source of the issue. As we try to fix our thinking problems with more thinking, anxiety, stress, depression, obsession, overwhelm, or self-loathing keep raining down like a never-ending storm. The reason we can't overcome these feelings is that we think the problems are *out there*—and we think we can fix them if we just had more time to think.

The Happiest Right-Brained People on the Planet

The last remaining members of the Pirahã Tribe (about eight hundred people who call themselves the Hi'aiti'ihi) live in the Amazon rainforest and until recently had no contact with the outside world. They are hunter-gatherers, so their way of life predates humanity's movement toward agricultural societies over twelve thousand years ago. Admirably, the Brazilian government has largely protected the Pirahã from outsiders' influence, so they continue to live with little interaction with the outside world.

Former missionary turned professor of linguistics Daniel Everett spent many years living with the Pirahã, initially in an effort to convert them to Christianity. He reported that in all the years he spent trying to convert members of the tribe, he never had one successful conversion to Christianity, and, in the end, he ended up leaving Christianity as a result of what he learned from them.

If we look at the culture and behavior of the Pirahã through the lens of neuroscience, especially in what we know about the differences between the left and right sides of the brain, they stand out as singular among world cultures. Unlike in our society, the Pirahã do not appear to be dominated by the tendencies of the left brain, and this is why I refer to them as the happiest right-brained people on the planet.

Most notably, according to Everett and others who have interacted with the Pirahã, they live almost entirely in the present moment. In fact, they have almost no use for the past except as it pertains to personal experience that might be helpful in the present.

Furthermore, they have no use for storytelling, including any story about God or a creation myth of any kind. When Everett asked them about how the Amazon jungle came to be, their response was basically, "I don't know, it's just here." As you read this, you may hear your own left brain revolting at the simplicity or uselessness of that answer. But is it really a "wrong" explanation?

This lack of interest in storytelling provided one of Everett's biggest challenges when it came to converting these people to Christianity. When he told them about Jesus, they asked Everett to describe what Jesus looked like, and quickly realized that he had never met him. They then assumed that someone Everett knew had met Jesus, and when they learned that no one he knew had ever seen or met Jesus, they quickly dismissed the entire story as useless. They couldn't understand why anyone would believe something that they hadn't personally witnessed or heard from someone who personally witnessed it. Their connection to the present moment was powerful and practical.

Furthermore, the Pirahã have no formal leaders or social hierarchy. No one in the tribe gets to tell anyone else what to do. They reject any categorizations of the kind that would give status to some over others. To our own left brains this might sound like chaos, or naivete, but those who have visited them almost all remark how happy and brilliant this group seems to be.

Most notably, they don't use numbers, a favorite abstraction so ubiquitous in the West it's hard to imagine life without it. They have concepts for things like "a few" or "many" but counting and math aren't necessary for them. Everett makes clear that this isn't some cognitive incapacity, as they are like an encyclopedia of knowledge regarding their surroundings. "They can walk into the jungle naked, with no tools or weapons, and walk out three days later with baskets of fruit, nuts, and small game."[34]

While many of us believe a new car or house will improve our happiness, the Pirahã, in spite of having almost no material goods in the sense that we think of them, do not want anything they do not already have. Everett has explained that when Westerners would try to tempt them with things that would "make their lives easier" they would decline, replying with something like, "You almost make me want this." In a mirror of Buddhism's main teaching that desire is the source of suffering, the Pirahã seem to embody "no desire, no suffering" without having read any sutras. After dealing with outsiders from the tribe they gave us all a collective name: "crooked heads." Very telling, and arguably quite accurate.

The most unique quality of the Pirahã is their language, which employs very few distinct consonant and vowel sounds but has many variations of intonation, and the length and stressing of syllables. This means that speakers can sing, hum, or even whistle their language, often using it to communicate across far distances. Perhaps more than anything, this points to a right brain dominance in their worldview. You probably already know that when a person has a stroke in their left brain, it is common for them to lose the ability to speak, because most language areas are housed in the left brain. However, this same stroke patient who cannot talk can often sing, because music and singing are housed in the right brain. In fact, Western medicine has undergone a major shift in dealing with stroke patients. Rather than asking patients to use damaged areas of the left brain to speak, many are now taught to communicate using song.

The Pirahã use different tones in a complex system of articulation. The same word can have a different meaning when pronounced in different tones. Western speakers do this sometimes (sarcasm is a common example), but neuroscience has discovered that this skill is lost when the right brain is damaged.

In learning about this tribe, I have been inspired to think about ways that anyone can practice detaching from the left brain's obsession with categorization, numerical thinking, and stories of the past. The exercises that follow are designed to help you try out experiencing the world more holistically and integrating the self with the world in the present moment.

Exercise: Imagine Life without Social Categories

The Pirahã have no social categories, and it's considered very bad manners to tell anyone what to do because no person belongs to a social category that is above or below another. Have you ever asked yourself why some people in your culture are allowed to tell other people what to do? There are many nuances in the core social hierarchies across the world, and this doesn't have to be a criticism. Every category can be useful if we remember what it is—just a tool, not reality. We think of social categories in physical terms. The people "above" you can tell you what to do, and you can tell the people "below" you what to do. But of course there is nothing in physical reality that gives anyone the authority to tell others what to do outside of the social categories constructed by the left brain. Hierarchies of this kind have allowed the many to be ruled by the few for most of the history of human civilizations. To the Pirahã, this is ridiculous.

Try it on for yourself and imagine if social categories disappeared tomorrow. Spend one day being hyperaware of any time you ask someone else to do something, or someone tells you to do something. Reflect on the ways that control isn't always obvious. What would it mean to step away from controlling or being controlled for a single day, or longer? Would you act differently? Feel differently? Why?

Exercise: A Day without Any Stories of the Past

The Pirahã have no interest in the past or the future and are one of the few groups that live in the present moment as a matter of culture. Could you live for a day like this? Try it. Try to go an entire day without talking about the past or the future in any way. (Talking about the past may be useful at work, so you may have to try this out on a day off.) You will no doubt continue to think about the past and future, so just aim for not talking about it with anyone else. See how this makes you feel.

If you slip up, don't worry—just make a quick note of it on your phone or a notepad. Consider if it affects your thinking at all, or your sense of self. It can be quite challenging and enlightening to explore how reliant we are on abstract concepts that take us out of the present moment.

Think of your story as luggage you are carrying around. While it can be useful to bring things with you, it can also feel freeing to release all this heavy stuff and explore without it. You have been carrying your self-story now for so many years you've probably forgotten what it feels like to put it down. Can you simply be where you are, when you are, without a story? This is the art of mindfulness.

Exercise: Notice All the Ways the Mind Uses Numbers

The Pirahã do not use numbers. Consider how radical this is. Numbers are at the core of many categorical processes of the left brain. For instance, how do we know who is rich unless we count money, cars, and houses? Who is a star athlete but the one with the most awards and the best stats? Notice our dependence on numbers as they relate to time. What time did you get up this morning? What year is it? What month is it? If you woke up from a coma and couldn't access a clock or a calendar, you would feel totally lost.

Furthermore, many of us live in a strange matrix of time and money, whether we get paid an annual salary for a forty-hour week or have an hourly rate for the hours we work. Even the fictitious self depends on an age that's based on how many times our rock has circled the sun since our birth. Your weight, number of siblings, number of lifetime sexual partners, net worth, and so many more numbers are abstractions that contribute to your sense of self. The Pirahã have no use for any of this; these fictions are not part of their reality and they are perhaps far happier for it.

For this practice, spend a day becoming more conscious of how much attention and credence you give to numbers. As you do, notice that most numbers represent categorization in overdrive. Whenever a number pops up in your head or out in the world, or you find yourself counting, noticing a price, or wondering about the time, take a breath and find yourself again in the now. See the number for what it is: an abstraction created by the left brain.

Imagine the day of the Pirahã. Their world has none of these fictions. You might even try politely declining some of these numerical fictions, just as members of the tribe turned down modern time-saving machines: "You almost make me want this."

Connecting with the Earth

The Pirahã tribe, living as hunter-gatherers in the Amazon jungle, are connected to the physical earth in a way few of us have ever experienced. Interestingly, there is a line of research showing that our left brain processes nonliving, mechanical things (cars, concrete, homes, dishes), while the right side of our brain processes the organic, living objects and aspects of our reality (plants, animals, faces, earth, ocean, sky, etc.)[35] And it's not just because of how these things look. Even in research subjects who have been blind since birth, these living and nonliving objects are processed by different regions of the brain. In some indigenous languages, such as Potawatomi, this distinction between the natural world and human-made things is baked into the grammar itself. Natural things are active doers, not inanimate objects. For example, the word for *lake* means "water making the form of a lake."

Remember the left brain controls the right side of the body and the right brain controls the left side of the body. About 80 percent of the world is right-hand dominant, and some neuroscientists have speculated if this reflects the dominance of the left brain that excels at manipulating the things in the world by using what it controls: the right hand. I wonder if the Pirahã people have the same level of right-hand dominance. As far as I know this has never been researched, but I speculate they do not.

In the last two thousand years, we started "protecting" ourselves from nature by becoming isolated from it while at the same time believing we were masters over it. Over the most recent generations, "protecting" ourselves from nature has become an ever-increasing priority that humans have tackled through new technologies and innovations. We put rubber soles on our shoes in the name of comfort and safety, as well as to protect ourselves from human-made sewage and trash. We built complex structures from human-made materials and live most of our lives indoors. Yet these practices have isolated us from the earth. Our feet evolved to be connected to the earth. We evolved to sleep on the earth, or very near it. Yet modern mechanical advances steadily pull us away from these physical earth connections.

With all of these "improvements," we cut ourselves off from the Earth's energy and the benefits of its negative electric charge, which some researchers are finding has anti-inflammatory and healing effects.[36] At the same time, we have surrounded ourselves with a plethora of positive electrical changes from our phones, tablets, TVs, and "smart" homes. We have cut off the normal, life-giving exchange of particles between us and the earth. Remember, on a molecular level, we are just thinking stardust. Our bodies are electrical-chemical systems made from the same energy that makes up every other thing in the galaxy. After millions of years of living in balance with the earth's energy, we have taken a radical turn away from balance.

I find it fascinating that some Indigenous tribes from the Americas would say that if you wear shoes, you will become sick, and it was common to cure a sickness by digging a hole and letting the person heal by having direct contact with the earth.[37] The science has backed up many of these intuitive insights. Having a direct connection with the earth, called "grounding," thins the blood after only two hours, has a dramatic effect on reducing inflammation, and has an even more interesting effect on the brain.[38] One recent study found that simply connecting back with the earth by walking barefoot or sitting on the ground had an immediate effect on the electrical activity of the left brain but had no effect on the right brain.[39] In other words, getting back to nature is one way of turning down the volume of the thinking mind. We've known for a long time that nature walks renew the soul; but now, thanks to the brain-measuring techniques in cognitive science, we have at least a basic idea of why this is.

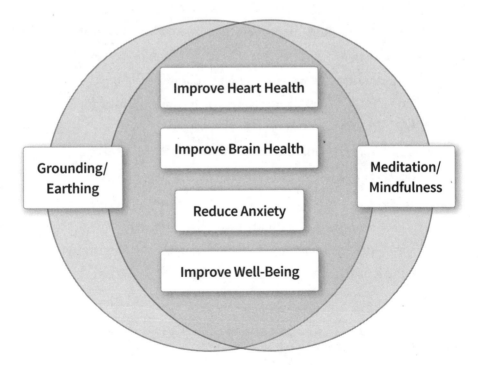

Practice: Get the Shoes Off and Walk the Earth

When was the last time you walked on the earth barefoot? If you asked me this very question as recently as last year, I would need to go all the way back to childhood (except for occasional walks on the beach, where it is still culturally acceptable to walk without shoes). Today, I make it a practice to walk on the earth with my bare feet as much as possible. I also introduce this practice to others in the mindfulness course I teach, and the results are always immediate, and mind-blowing. People relate having the sensation of uplifting the soul and turning down the overthinking mind. For many people, they have had shoes on for so long that taking them off is like getting a whole new sense activated. Like cataract surgery to clear their foggy vision. It's like they have just opened their eyes for the first time.

Now it's your turn. Stop reading, take your shoes off, and go walk on some bare earth for thirty minutes. Breathe deeply as you do so and be conscious that you are breathing. Don't skip this practice, even if your mind deems it "too simple" or "not meaningful." Write down what you experience. Try to connect with the earth in this way a couple times per week if possible.

The Mind Hides from Itself

I believe that despite its amazing discoveries, cognitive science has missed the most important quality of this left-brain module: its ability to hide, even from itself. Once again, we can recall the definition of *cognition*, which acknowledges that the mind doesn't perceive actual reality. But this misses the point that the person having the thought absolutely believes that cognition *is* an accurate reflection of reality. The mind is hiding from itself. In the

Advaita Vedanta school of Hindu philosophy, the word *Maya* refers to an illusion that keeps us from experiencing the real nature of our existence.

By the time the word *Maya* was being translated into the European languages it was defined as the illusory dream world that we call physical reality, but the concept may actually be closer to the process of "thinking" itself. The ancients used the term Maya to describe the Gods' ability to construct illusory forms from nothing. As we have discussed throughout this book, this is exactly what the thinking mind does: it makes stuff up.

Take a quick look and notice the world around you. It *appears* to have color, depth, and motion. The sounds you hear seem to be *out there* in a reality external to you. But what is clear from modern neuroscience is that our experience only exists as a neural event in our skull. Everything you see is just a neural representation, and yet we believe we are directly experiencing the world as it is. It's similar to the goal of every stage magician, to make us believe through illusion and misdirection that what we think we are seeing is really happening. When we become aware, however, of how the trick is done—when we learn how to see how the magician palms a coin or holds a card behind their open hand—we become more acutely aware of ourselves and our relationship to the performance on stage.

Exercise: A Simple Observation

Find a single flower to observe. A flower appears to have depth, shape, and color. Of course, your brain has no direct experience of this flower. Rather, all it knows is the information from the light energy that has reflected off it and is then processed by your brain.

The depth, shape, color, and movement are contained within this light energy, which the brain interprets. We experience the interpretation, not the flower itself.[40] The trick of Maya is to mistake our thoughts and neural representations about the flower for the flower itself.

Next, consider the depth of the flower. As you look at it, it has three dimensions. That is, it isn't flat like a picture. Parts of it are closer to you and other parts are farther away, hidden in shadow. The retina, at the back of the eye, can represent width and length, but it has no way to directly encode depth, so the brain must create an illusion of depth.

If you hold a finger just in front of your nose and close and open one eye at a time, you will see that each eye gets a slightly different view of the world. These two slightly different views are combined to create an illusion of depth. The more different the two images, the closer the object appears. The less different the two images, the farther away it appears.

All the depth you are visually experiencing is not real depth, but rather a neural code of depth that we mistake as real. Neuroscientists have found special neurons called binocular (or two eye) neurons that process depth. If these neurons are damaged, the brain can no longer perceive depth. If they are stimulated in a particular way, an animal will respond to the depth corresponding to the neurons, not reality.

Now notice the flower's color. There is an area in the brain called V4, which processes color information. Isaac Newton once said that light waves have no color, and this is true, as color is manufactured by the brain. Light energy varies in wavelength (the distance between the peaks of two waves), and the brain creates the experience of different colors based on this.

A rainbow is an extraordinary example. This is the light energy from the sun being "broken apart" into different wavelengths we experience as violet, blue, green, yellow, orange, and red. Every color is the exact same sort of energy as it hits your eye and brain, only as you move from blue to red, can you distinguish that the wavelengths get longer. Outside of our ability to represent color in the brain, there is no color in the universe—only differences in the wavelength of light energy, which our brains have evolved to interpret as different colors. Without the brain, the only difference between red and green is that red has a longer wavelength. If V4 is damaged, these look the same shade of gray along with the rest of the colorless world.

Move the flower around; spin it in circles. Do you think that's motion you're perceiving? There is another brain area called V5 that processes motion and there are specialized neurons that process the directions an object is moving in. In the lab, if an animal is viewing an object moving "up" but the researchers stimulate the "down" cells, an animal will experience the object moving in a downward motion.

For the mind to be successful at its trick, it had to be hard-wired to make certain that the nature of thought was never questioned. Like the fish that doesn't perceive the water it's swimming in, we are so deep within the mind that most of us never notice it.

The trick of Maya is to make neural processing not seem like neural processing but actual reality. When it comes to looking at a flower, it may not make a difference to anyone that our representations of color, depth, or motion are just neural representations, as they may still be beautiful. Yet there's a whole Maya, or thinking-based, world of problems: bills, traffic jams, difficult coworkers, drama, and frustrations that create most modern suffering. If these are realized for what they are, if we can see the trick of Maya in the hands of the thinking mind magician, we can profoundly alter our relationship to this suffering.

The Stress of Stressful Thoughts

Kelly McGonigal's Ted Talk "How to Make Stress Your Friend" is an excellent example of how beliefs are wired into our body and even reality itself. In this talk, she discusses a study that had thousands of subjects and measured things that are stressful and variables about health. The most interesting finding was that stress predicted poor health, as expected, but only for those who believed that stress is bad for you! For the subjects who didn't believe that stress was bad, the stress responses didn't appear to be related to any negative health issues. That is, the stressors themselves were not the problem; rather, the belief and identification with the illusions around the stressors created the suffering.

Here are some questions to ponder.

- How can a thought change the nervous system and affect our health?

- If thoughts are just abstractions that are disconnected from reality, how do they affect reality?

Stress itself isn't a bad thing. In fact, the body and nervous system evolved to use stress as a tool for survival, a shortcut that ramps up certain systems in the body to keep us safe. Yet the thinking mind, in its efforts to remember, categorize, and predict, can't let go even long after the threat has passed. Here we are, stuck with ruminating, stressful thoughts, including the thought that "stress is bad." Those thoughts then keep the cycle of stress response going in the body, flooding us nonstop with stress hormones and wearing down our immune system and other biological processes, resulting in worse health outcomes over time.

Can you see how our thinking about stress is now the problem? Are you getting a feel for how the unending game of Maya works? It's always an inside job. Happiness, stress, and peace of mind are all inner processes.

There is an interesting avenue of trauma therapy developed by Dr. Peter Levine called Somatic Experiencing, which draws inspiration from observations of certain kinds of physical animal behaviors that process and release stress. You've probably noticed that in response to a perceived threat, cats' and dogs' fur will stand on end along their spine. When the threat has passed, the animal will do a full-body shake, releasing the tension and resetting the nervous system. But this energy in humans very often gets pent up.

In something like post-traumatic stress disorder, or PTSD, the body and the mind work together to trap a person in a nonstop cycle of re-experiencing stressors in memories and flashbacks. This nonstop cycle of exposure to the memory of trauma wears down the nervous system and degrades one's health and well-being. The amazing thing about Somatic Experiencing is that the therapist doesn't even need to know the story causing the pain. They can bypass the thinking mind altogether and home in on the physical (often unconscious) manifestations of trauma, retraining the body to undo its effects with simple breathing and movement exercises.

Mental Imagery: The Mind's Eyes and Ears

Mental imagery allows us to engage in our favorite hobby of daydreaming—that is, imagining being someplace we are not and doing something other than what we are really doing. Rather than waiting in a traffic jam, we take our virtual reality flight to the beach or imagine the perfect comeback to the last time we got into a debate. In evolutionary terms, the advantage of this inner theater was that it made use of any available downtime to work on the problem of survival in the mind's eye rather than in the higher stakes realm of reality.

Back in the eighties, psychology was desperately trying to figure out how we conjure up these images; but it was Stephen Kosslyn, a well-known cognitive scientist, who put the question to rest. In a series of experiments, Kosslyn was able to show that in order to form a visual mental image, you employ the visual processing part of the brain.[41] Here is a simple demonstration of visual mental imagery.

Exercise: Visual Mental Imagery

Close your eyes and imagine the smallest letter A that you can. Then imagine it twice as big. Keep doubling its size in your imagination until it is too large to fit your inner screen.

Kosslyn's research found that each time you make the image in your mind larger, the activity in the visual part of your brain increases. Your internal visual theater functions via your *actual* visual system. When you see with your mind's eye, you are using the same system that creates real vision by responding to light waves. From the brain's perspective, it doesn't really matter if you are really looking at a letter A or just forming the image in the mind; both experiences are made from the same neural building blocks.

Athletes are taught to imagine taking a shot in their mind's eye before they actually do it, and there's solid research to show that performing in your mind first improves actual performance. Mental imagery changes the brain and affects our body for one simple reason: the brain cannot distinguish its representations from reality because representations are all the brain has ever known. If there is a real world, your brain has never known it. Not directly.

The brain's three pounds has floated around in its protective skull since its inception, never knowing the touch of a real flower, the smell or taste of real coffee, or the vastness of the real night sky. All it has ever known is what it has represented and interpreted about the flower, the coffee, and the sky in the form of neurons that receive information from the outside world.

Maya has pulled the wool over your eyes (or brain, in this case). All this time, you believe you've been seeing reality, when what you've really been seeing is just an interpretation, a representation, of reality. As I said, it's all an inside job.

Practice: Let the Sunshine In

This practice works best on a nice, sunny day. Go outdoors and turn your face toward the sun, letting it feel the sunlight. Recall that the energy hitting your face left the sun eight minutes ago and traveled all the way through space (at the speed of light, of course) to reach you and produce that feeling of warmth. More light from the sun is bouncing off everything all around you, enabling you to see the trees, buildings, sidewalks, water. That light energy is making contact with your eyes and illuminating your world. No wonder the phrase "Let there be light" is so powerful. Without light we would be floating in nothingness.

In my sensation and perception class, I lecture on a process called transduction. This is the process by which energy from the outside world is translated into a neural language the brain can understand. When it comes to light, a particle of light (called a photon) interacts with a light-sensitive cell in the eye, and eventually the brain will give rise to the experience of light. The word *transduction* sounds technical and scientific, but it is in fact a mystical term. Transduction is a total mystery. Not only are physicists still unsure about *what light is,* exactly, but no one has a clue how the process of transduction takes place. Regardless, we do know that no one ever actually "sees" a particle of light—at least not directly. All we ever experience about light is what the nervous system experiences after the light-sensitive cell in the eye has taken in the information from this particle and the brain has decoded it.

It's not hard to make the next logical conclusion, which is that light itself isn't really light. That's how powerful Maya is. The only light is inside your skull as your experience! Even on the brightest, sunniest day, all that light is inside your head, not out in reality. That is, these particles only carry information about our environment that interacts with brain cells in a mysterious act of information exchange. This information "lights up" the visual brain in an otherwise dark universe by providing information. This is not how we typically think of light, or seeing.

Until now, you have probably said "It's bright outside" or even "I need to turn the light on in the room so I can see," as if the light itself had brightness to it. What if, rather than light, it is in fact clear consciousness that illuminates the universe?

For eons, humans have used light as a comfortable metaphor for knowledge and insight. If someone is "kept in the dark," they are ignorant of information. If someone "sees the light," they have come into a new understanding. Because light is only inside the mind, light is the same as knowledge and insight. Both are describing consciousness itself. Martin Luther King Jr. once said, "Darkness cannot drive out darkness; only light can do that."[42] Carl Jung intoned, "As far as we can discern, the sole purpose of human existence is to kindle a light in the darkness of mere being."[43] To see and perceive the world around us, we need to be informed. We need the lights on.

This connection between light and knowing goes deeper.

Desire

The Buddha uncovered the secrets of the thinking mind that we've been exploring in this book around twenty-five hundred years ago. Upon realizing how the thinking mind works, the Buddha gave a lecture that outlined how the mind gives rise to suffering:

1. Much of life is mental suffering.

2. Suffering is caused by desire.

He then went on to teach that the ability to release desire could lead to an experience of radical content with the way things are. Of course, those with desire are more likely to explore, invent, and seek out improvements over the way things are. This desire drives the creation of civilizations, shopping malls, mass transit, space travel, and medical science. But why do we still want more, even after we've arguably provided ourselves with the means to live a long and relatively comfortable life? Will we ever stop? The truth is that we won't; if we allow the thinking mind to govern our lives, no matter how good it gets there will be no end to the search for something better.

Practice: What Do You Want?

Left unchecked, the thinking mind will scan for ways to avoid suffering by creating and then trying to fix problem after problem. This is what the thinking mind evolved to do. There's nothing wrong with it. However, if you are not in physical pain, you have a roof over your head and access to food and clean water, you don't really *need* anything else. So beyond those needs, make a list of your current top wants. Do you want a new house? A new car? A new job? A million dollars? Do you want to lose weight? Do you want someone special to love you? Do you want enlightenment?

Once you've made your list, don't judge yourself for it. It's fine to want things; it's what the mind does. Next, consider whether the mind is using any of these items on the list to enhance its sense of self. Will you "be somebody" if you have a new house or car, a million dollars, or enlightenment? This is where desire and Maya intersect, as the mind uses desire and illusion to perpetuate its own imaginary existence. Now, consider what part of you can realize this. It's not the thinking mind.

Make a practice of bringing clear consciousness to your present state, just as it is. If you can see that your needs are met and any wants beyond that are contributing to a desire/suffering feedback loop, you have created some space between your true self and the thinking mind.

Practice: Mindful Eating

Have you ever gotten a carton of ice cream from the freezer, sat down with a spoon, and only a few minutes later noticed the carton was empty? Ever ordered a pizza and then eaten the whole thing before you realized it? It wasn't *you* who ate that whole pizza—it was the mind. Some minds turn on and eat until they cannot take another bite, without any awareness of what's happening outside the mind. For our ancestors, a mind that urged us to eat like this wasn't a real problem. Consider the benefit of finding a fig tree and eating past the point of satiation—someone might come across this bounty once a year, not every day. Eating is another area where desire and Maya intersect.

Many people have unlimited access to processed foods, which are engineered in a lab to have some combination of salt, sugar, fat, and texture that is irresistible to taste buds and to the mind. Furthermore, our thinking minds would often rather put our chewing and swallowing on autopilot in favor of the attention-grabbing devices in front of us. All of this contributes to the obesity epidemic we find ourselves in today.

Mindful eating is a practice that works with the need and desire to eat and introduces a way to bring more clear consciousness to our meals. Besides making eating more pleasurable, mindful eating can reset the body's natural ability to regulate food intake independent of the chatterbox mind.

With mindful eating we slow down and become conscious of each moment. We tap into the sensory experience of a meal. The look, smell, mouthfeel, taste, and even sounds of chewing our food contributes to the overall experience. In my class, I ask students to practice thirty minutes of mindful eating at lunch. Because most meals these days happen around something else as the focus of our awareness (the phone, TV, conversation), it can feel strange to really pay attention to our food. For many of my students, this is the *first time* they've been fully conscious of what they are eating.

If thirty minutes feels like too much to start with, I invite you to be mindful of the first bite of each meal for the next couple days. Take some time to smell your food, to look at it. If you can put it in your hands and feel it, that is also an interesting experience. Take the first bite and notice all the flavors as you slowly chew and swallow. If you want to experiment with a mindful second bite, go for it.

Habituation

Habituation, or "getting used to things," is one of the most basic forms of learning known in the biological sciences. This is our hardwired tendency to experience a decreasing response to repeated stimuli. Habituation doesn't have to be taught; all beings with a nervous system do it automatically, and it's one of the first and most basic survival tools. We experience this every day. Habituation describes what happens when we stop noticing the sound and vibration of the heater, or when we no longer notice the feeling of our shoes or clothes after we put them on.

The mind evolved to prioritize what it believes to be new. This simple subroutine in the mind results in much of what we know as mental suffering. When dealing with losses, habituation provides a great advantage. However, it backfires in terms of dealing with the gains.

In a now famous experiment, a subject's overall well-being was measured after a huge loss (becoming physically paralyzed) or a huge gain (winning the lottery).[44] After a very short time, both the gain and the loss came to feel normal to the person who experienced it. That is, after a while, the well-being of both groups became similar. So, if you win millions, in a short time you will get used to it and you will return to your normal tendency to desire things you do not have, and bemoan problems. However, if you suffer a great loss, the mind will also become used to this, which can be a life-saving comfort. The sting of even the most catastrophic loss can be borne thanks to habituation. No matter what happens, good or bad, both will eventually come to feel normal.

This can make being a billionaire feel normal the same way it can make prison feel normal. Combine the mind's ability to normalize anything with desire, and together they create a perfect storm for suffering. The thinking mind always wants more, but when it gets more, it is soon bored with what it has, and it wants more all over again. The cycle continues, on and on.

Practice: Doing Nothing

For the next two minutes, do nothing. Put down this book, set a timer on your phone, and just sit. Don't try to meditate. Don't try to do anything. Just sit. There is nothing to do and no place to go.

How did that feel? Did you feel impatient, restless, bored? Perhaps you were at peace. If so, that's wonderful. One study found that some people would rather give themselves an electric shock than do nothing but sit with their own thoughts.[45] If you felt restless, or noticed that the mind was looking for "what's next" or reliving the past, there is no need to see it as a personal problem. It is just an example of the thinking mind. The next time you try doing two minutes of nothing, you can give yourself gentle reminders to "do less" and then "do even less." If two minutes of doing nothing seems like an eternity, try a smaller move first, like thirty seconds.

The thinking mind didn't evolve to stay satisfied with anything for very long, so one of its favorite tricks is to push away from the present, into the past or the future. But is there really anything wrong with this moment? Or is the mind only trying to tell us there is? Mini breaks of nothing can build the mind's tolerance for the present moment, in which things are very rarely wrong.

We have a thinking problem we are trying to think our way out of. This doesn't work. The only way we can work on this "problem" is by becoming aware of the thinking mind and becoming less identified with it. We can do this by exposing the left brain's tendencies toward bias, storytelling, and laziness. We can also build up certain abilities and tendencies of the right brain to playfully challenge, surprise, or inspire us toward more happiness and well-being.

Mind Check

At this point let's explicitly and consciously assess the extent that you have come to recognize the mind. Maybe you still hear the voice in your head, but I hope by now that it feels more like you are listening rather than talking. For some people, it can produce a little anxiety to realize that the voice in your head isn't really you.

That's okay—this anxiety is only arising from more mind activity. The more you recognize the mind, the easier it is to create space between the mind—and its clouds of ruminating, categorization, and abstract thinking—and clear consciousness.

At the same time, do not expect the mind to change simply because you are identifying less with it. You are not trying to change your mind! That's not possible. You can, however, change your relationship to the thinking mind, and this is great news. Your life will change and the mind will keep running its inflexible, predictable computer program. No amount of awareness will change a computer program. But awareness can certainly allow you to stand up and walk into another room to get a little space while the computer toils away at its self-generated tasks. Your awareness that the mind is just doing its thing allows you to open all sorts of doors to other rooms.

Perhaps instead of the idea that we can "change our mind" we can use the expression "I'm not my mind" to remember that we no longer have to let the voice in our head dictate our lives. There is a world of difference between living controlled by the program and living with the awareness of it, and we can use our language to remind us of this.

Of course, you can't think your way to this awareness. You have to experience it. I'd like to look at a few ways to access this experience, and a few exercises that can help bring the right brain into balance as well. After all, we only have one portal to existence, this pesky mind, but we can certainly learn how to explore, play, create, and imagine within its confines.

Balance

Walking down the street, standing on one leg, playing almost any sport—all of these depend on our physical ability to balance. The brain has a complex, largely nonthinking system for maintaining balance in the body. In fact, becoming conscious and starting to "think" about balance can often trip it up. (Pun intended.) We can easily keep our balance walking a rope when it is laying on the ground, but string it up in the air and the thinking mind turns on and we quickly lose our balance.

Of course, balance extends beyond the physical realm into the more metaphorical ideas of balancing work and play, rest and exercise, and dozens of other variables in life. In these arenas as well, when we favor the thinking mind over bodily knowing, we can tip far out of balance in any number of directions.

In Taoism, the ancient yin-yang symbol shows the interrelatedness of all things. This symbol is a visual reminder that anything the mind has categorized into "opposites" is based on perception, not reality. Yin-yang shows the delicate way in which two things that seem to be opposites balance each other out and are interconnected. That is, opposites are not enemies but cooperative friends.

The thinking mind created imbalance because imbalance is purely perceptual. Nothing can be out of balance unless you decide that "balance" looks different than what you are currently seeing or experiencing. Think of a crooked picture on the wall. It isn't "crooked" until a mind looks at it and sees that it is imbalanced. It isn't imbalanced until there is the thought and judgment that it is so. Until then, it's just part of the harmonious flow of the universe, like everything else.

It's like that old question, If a tree falls in the forest and no one is around to hear it, does it make a sound? If there is a picture on the wall but no mind to judge that it is crooked, is it really crooked at all? The balancing act of the universe involves far too many variables for the thinking mind to think about. This was the insight of the early Taoists.

Integration

The root of the word *integration* is from a Latin word meaning "to make whole" or "to bring together the parts of." Now that we have an awareness that we are not the thinking mind, we can embrace the goal of integrating the whole mind. We don't want to (and couldn't if we tried) discard all the functions of the left brain. We can, however, integrate them into the totality of our being.

One way to sum up the vast majority of Eastern teachings would be to say, "You are not the voice in your head." For most people, this teaching alone can bring about significant change in their inner and outer life, moving away from drama and toward great peace.

However, Taoism teaches that this is only partly true. You may have to separate your idea of self from the thinking mind in order to move toward integration, just as you might separate an egg yolk from its white in a recipe before mixing them back together into the whole. Furthermore, nature didn't create the left and right brain as separate organs, but rather built a bridge of 800 million nerve fibers connecting them.

So let this be your warning that integration may be like a Zen puzzle. Saying you are not the thinking mind isn't exactly true. The thinking mind is an important part of the whole dance of reality. This is the clear consciousness we talked about: the electricity that powers the computer is you, and so is the program running in the computer.

When you first experience that the left brain thinking mind isn't who you are, it can feel like putting down heavy luggage you've been carrying around for most of your life. For the rest of our journey together, we will explore how the real you has always been hiding successfully in the thinking mind. Now that we've lost our mind, it is time to put it all back together.

Balance without Control

What happens when you are told not to think about something? Let's try it. Once you read the bullet point below, try to spend about fifteen seconds not thinking about the proposed subject.

- Do *not* think of the number 13.

- Do *not* think of an elephant.

Successful? Probably not. Things only get worse when you feel real pressure to not think about something. One of the mechanisms rarely noticed by cognitive scientists or even psychologists is one of the most obvious, and it all has to do with balance. The mind doesn't know this, and it is precisely because the mind is ignorant of this that it can get so frustrated.

The thinking mind of course evolved from the mechanisms of the body and nervous system. These systems engage in nonstop acts of balance and regulation in ways that the thinking mind cannot begin to comprehend. Imagine if you had to "think through" how to digest an apple. Or how to fall asleep. Or the mechanics of running. When the thinking mind tries to insert itself in balancing and regulation, or tries to control its own processes, it can result in an enormous amount of frustration and anxiety.

The thinking mind's version of trying to keep balance can often create conflict. See if you have experienced any of the below forms of mental suffering:

- If you have the thought *I need to get to sleep*, the mind keeps you up all night. When the mind thinks you need to stay awake to watch a movie or pay attention to a lecture, you fall right to sleep.

- If the mind tries not to worry, it seems as if worrying is all you can do.

- If you think *I don't want to look nervous* before a talk, it is likely that you will become even more anxious. If someone tells you to "just be yourself," you suddenly forget who that is and present a limited, constricted version of you.

- In a sport, when you think *I need to make this next point,* you are likely to make a mistake that you otherwise would never make.

In each case, one could say that the thinking mind tries to take over and manage a high-stakes situation by controlling it. And yet balance is almost never achieved through control, at least not for very long. It just doesn't work.

Instead of using controlling effort to push things around in your skull, try the Taoist practice of *wu wei*, which means no effort. Controlling the mind leads to the mind attempting a balancing response: don't think/can't stop thinking; don't mess up/higher chance of messing up. *Wu wei* stops the process before it starts. Do less. And then less than that. Notice what happens when you don't try to control the outcome. You might find yourself in a kind of harmonious balance.

Practice: Drop the Doing

If I asked you what you have to do today, this week, this month, or this year, no doubt you would be able to give me a list in a matter of moments.

What if I waved a magic wand that made every single one of these "have to do" items vanish (with no negative consequences)? There is nowhere you need to go, no agenda, no pressing appointments, and no one counting on you. You probably are already feeling a mild panic rising in your chest. The magic wand takes care of that too. *Poof!*

Some people feel that if they didn't have anything they had to do, nothing would ever get done. They think their lives will grind to a halt or that they'll never get out of bed in the morning. Sounds like left-brained panic to me. Another way I like to think about this is to answer the question, What would you be doing right now if success was assured, and money was no object? Really think about this. Imagine it.

Whatever your answer, consider it a clue to a deeper want from your clear consciousness. You don't have to do anything about that deeper want, but you might get inspired to action in a way that feels very different than your to-do list. Even if this deeper want doesn't feel possible for you right now, you also don't have to listen to the naysayer left brain either. Release the need to always be doing.

Distraction Therapy

Tourette's syndrome is characterized by involuntary movements or vocalizations called tics. It is very common for parents of children with Tourette's to report that after their child has spent the day at school doing their best to suppress their tics, the moment they come home there is an explosion of tics. The more a patient tries to suppress a tic, the worse it gets.

However, neurologist Oliver Sacks tells the story of a surgeon with Tourette's who would display many of the typical symptoms but could remain symptom-free while performing surgery.[46] As long as his attention wasn't interrupted, he remained free of tics. In other words, when the surgeon's attention was completely fixed somewhere else, his mind never stepped in to try to "fix" things. I call this distraction therapy; it works because it distracts the mind from using effort or control.

Have you ever frozen up or "choked" at the very moment you really needed to perform your best? Were you ever in a situation in which you tried hard for a particular outcome but it backfired? It was almost as if it was the "trying too hard" that messed everything up. Ancient wisdom teachers knew very well that when one tries too hard, one will fail, because the mind has insisted on a particular outcome.

One remedy for this tendency of the mind is to take "trying" and replace it with acceptance instead. Or we can put it this way: There are really two ways to fail. You can fail poorly, or you can fail gracefully. You can run from failing, or you can jump into it.

So rather than the mind struggling with the insistence of "I must not fail," work to fully embrace the possibility of failure as much as you would success.

Because it's the mind, and particularly the left brain, that is insisting on a particular outcome, when you no longer try to control the outcome, you are no longer in conflict with the mind. You accept every outcome because you know that you are not in control.

Practice: Allowing and Accepting

Have you ever avoided having a difficult conversation with your partner, only to have a big blow-out fight about something trivial? There's an old saying with a lot of truth in it: whatever you resist, persists. Try this practice to allow emotions and thoughts to take their natural course and move through the body.

Left-brain attempts to control the body or emotions often sound something like this: *I need to go to sleep right now; I'm nervous about my meeting at work tomorrow and I don't want to be; I don't have any right to be angry.* Perhaps there's a memory you keep reliving and you wish it would go away. Or a feeling of regret you can't seem to change. These often take the form of the left brain saying, "if only": *If only I hadn't said that; I'll be happy if only I can get this big promotion.*

Rather than trying to control the mind with left-brain verbal chatter, let the mind go where it goes. After all, it isn't you, your thoughts are not you, so why do you care where it goes? What if you just observe and accept rather than try to get in there and change it?

If the mind wants to be nervous before a talk, embrace the anxiety. If you feel shaky, shake your arms and legs. If the mind is embarrassed, dive deep into the embarrassment. Let your cheeks flush and tears well up in your eyes. Observe how it feels, and don't try to control or predict the outcome. Resist letting the left brain tell a story about your state, like, *I'm such a coward,* or *Will I ever learn?* If the mind wants to worry, let the worry flow.

Holocaust survivor, psychologist, and author of *Man's Search for Meaning* Viktor E. Frankl called this "paradoxical intention." In one case, a patient of his has trouble with excessive hand sweating, so Frankl tells him to intentionally sweat as much as he possibly can, which results in an almost immediate cure. Allowing and accepting often has a strange potency. When you dive into an unpleasant emotion, it often fades quickly. Running from embarrassment and not wanting others to know you are embarrassed *is* the embarrassment. If you own it, and even try to fuel it, it will fade quickly. This reflects one of the central insights into how the mind works, and why running from the mind has always created its own problems.

In the same way a sailor can use the wind to sail into the wind, the true self can learn to use the mind like the tool it was intended to be. There is an old Zen saying that water becomes still when left alone. When the mind tries to force things into balance, we end up in worse shape. We move the water. Trying not to worry creates more worry; suppressing anger instigates more anger. Remember, the mind is doing what it's made to do. It thinks just like the heart beats and the lungs breathe. But the mind isn't you. Knowing this takes away its power and allows you to relinquish the desire to control.

The Feeling Universe

While the mind may take credit for the heights of human culture, most of our experience of the world is driven by feelings. Animals were feeling for millions of years before humans started to think in anything resembling the way we do today. There is a lot of ongoing scientific inquiry into the subtle differences between body sensations, emotions, and thoughts. For some researchers, there is no way to distinguish between them at all. For our purposes, I think it is helpful to have some loose categories that some call IQ (intellectual knowing), EQ (emotional intelligence), and BQ (body or instinctual intelligence). These categories are totally made up by the thinking mind, of course, but they can help us understand some useful ways to work with our neurological system.

Like thoughts, emotions don't happen "to" us, but rather arise "from" us. In other words, just as we experience "seeing" because of the interaction of cells in our eyes and what gets relayed between those cells and our brain, the emotions we "feel" are very much a story created within the mind based on the information exchanged between our sensing organs and our brains.

Emotions give life meaning. They tend to help us make decisions faster and with more boldness. They are fundamental to the formation of our sense of self. They inform our social connections and familial bonds. They influence our health and well-being in profound ways.

Yet just as the thinking mind's faulty perceptions can lead us astray, our emotions sometimes seem to be pushing and pulling at us, particularly when they are under the spell of the thinking mind. Overwhelming or difficult emotions can begin to feel like a runaway horse. We struggle to hold on, and then once we fall off, our foot is caught in the stirrup, and we continue to be dragged. Oftentimes, the energy and pain of feeling emotions can be so acute that we'll do almost anything to avoid feelings altogether. Of course, suppressing emotions or numbing them can have unpredictable consequences. If we can more deeply understand the power of feelings, we can work with emotions in partnership rather than be dragged around behind the runaway horse.

In evolutionary terms, feelings let others know instantly what was going on through the tone of our voice, our body language, and our facial expressions. The vast majority of these basic emotional displays aren't subject to differences in geographical, social, or cultural location; they are hardwired into our brain and shared across cultures. Think of the expression of disgust at a bad smell, or the light in the eyes and broadening of the mouth of a genuine smile. These messages are meaningful no matter where you are on the planet.

Regardless of how much control the thinking mind has attempted to exert over them, emotions are still our main form of communication. The thinking mind just will not accept this. The next time you are talking with someone, say the exact same words but change their emotional content. Or take out all emotion altogether. You will get a very strange look. Six hundred million years of emotion will always be our foundation, even if we've added a thinking mind that trivializes its predecessor.

Cognitive science has proven that the thinking mind is limited to only one thought at a time. However, it's almost impossible to only have one feeling at a time. We have mixed feelings about almost everything. We even say, "Part of me feels this, but another part of me feels different." Our feelings change dramatically depending on any number of contextual factors. We can also be ambivalent, with varying levels of attachment to or identification with multiple conflicting emotions. The thinking mind avoids this chaotic landscape of feelings whenever it can. And yet, because emotions can reflect complexity and can change over time, they are in many ways a far more sophisticated decision-making tool than the thinking mind. This is why so many ancient traditions consider feelings to be far wiser than the thinking mind.

Distinguishing between Bias and Intuition

Feelings make our most important decisions for us, but the thinking mind would have us believe it's just the opposite. Because we are so culturally attuned to value the interpretive brain, we often have instant thoughts that "pop" into our heads (as we've explored throughout this book). These automatic thoughts might feel like intuition, but more than likely they are a way for the brain to skip over feelings altogether. In the case of bias, our thoughts dictate our feelings based on our imagined categorizations.

However, emotions are an older, more instinctual system in the brain than the thinking mind. If we learn how to become less identified with our thinking mind, our feelings will express an intelligence that far exceeds the survival concerns of the mind. Then we can return to feelings generating thoughts, which is a path that leads to better intuitive decision-making.

How do we get to a place where we can trust our intuition? Here are a few ways to get started.

Exercise: Where Do I Think? Where Do I Feel?

The renowned psychologist Carl Jung once met with a chief of the Taos pueblos, Ochwiay Biano (Mountain Lake). The elder commented that he didn't understand the Europeans: "The whites always want something; they are always uneasy and restless."

When Jung asked him why he thought they were like this, the elder said, "They say that they think with their heads."

"Why of course. What do you think with?" Jung replied.

"We think here," he said, indicating his heart.[47]

Think about a time when you were intensely happy or excited. Call up some of the basic details until you start to feel the emotion(s) in your body. Point to or rest your hands where you physically feel your feelings—it might be quickening breath, a flush in the cheeks, a restlessness in the legs.

Next, examine a thought—something particularly intellectual, like, *If A equals B and B equals C, does A equal C?* Think about this for a moment, and then point to where this thought is taking place in your body. Did you point to your head?

Virtually all wisdom teachings value feelings over thoughts, as long as the feelings are not out of fear. The mind grew out of the fear response system, but mistakes balance for opposition and gets caught up in a struggle of trying to control itself. To become aware of your emotions as they take place in your day-to-day life is to become the witness to your own experience. The more you practice and see how your thoughts are part of an inflexible program running in the thinking mind, the more you will see that you are *not* that program. You are something much, much bigger.

Practice: The Whole-Body Yes

Giving your mind, heart, and body what it is asking for is the foundation of a trusting relationship with yourself. The more trust you build, the more your body will give you clear yesses about meaningful questions. I call these whole-body yesses. You can use your yes to reinforce the feedback loop of your intuition.[48]

This will feel different for each person, so in order to find out what your whole-body yes is like, start with simple yes or no questions that are easy to answer and get a feel for the difference in thought, emotion, and physical sensation between a yes and a no.

- Do I want to start this direction for my morning walk? *Yes!*

- Do I want chicken for lunch? *No!*

- Would I like to see this movie? *Yes!*

Your internal yes may feel like a leaning forward energy, a lightness, a tingling in the hands and feet, or something else. Your thinking mind may be shouting yes in a verbal way, and your emotions may be anything from joy to fear to anger—all of these or any combination can provide the motivation for a strong yes. This is a kind of integration.

Once you get a whole-body yes, you must follow through on it. This is crucial. Similarly, if you get a "hit" of intuition—a strong, urgent sense that you should do something or avoid doing something, go with it. Write it down in case you can confirm your decision was a good one later. But regardless of whether you get "proof" after the fact, you're building up the muscle of being in tune with your own intelligence beyond the limits of the thinking mind.

In the West, there is little to no formal training of our intuitive capacities, which always take a back seat to the rationalizations of the thinking mind. We can train ourselves to use intuition to tap into the greater intelligence of the universe, or clear consciousness.

Sometimes you will get a partial yes. Then what? If your intellect is disagreeing with your emotions and your body, it's time to test your assumptions. Are you in a reactive mode? Are your thoughts trying to override valuable information coming from your emotions and your body? Are you willing to interrogate the "no" and see whether your reaction is based on fear or shame? Can you shift into a place of trusting your gut? At the very least, you can remind your thinking mind that nothing is certain—not even its own existence and connection to reality—so you might as well stay tuned to your intuition.

Practice: Uncover the Emotional Story

One way to work with our emotions is to uncover the story that we're telling about them. I had a friend who was going through a rough patch with her partner, and because she went through a previous divorce, she started to worry that maybe she was damaged goods, or, in her words, "the type that leaves people." Her thinking mind was making up a story about her identity based on underlying emotions that were difficult to sit with—fear of what she thought might happen, the pain and joy of being known by another person, the grief of losing independence within a relationship.

When we don't (or can't) check in with our bodies and emotions and uncover what's underneath a given story, we run the danger of entering an emotional loop. A familiar situation arises, certain feelings bubble up to the surface, and we behave in a certain reactionary way, over and over again. This can lead to questions about our identity, like, Why does this keep happening to me? or What kind of idiot would keep making this mistake?

The trick is that the body actually knows how to process emotions, as long as you can get the thinking mind to back off enough to let feelings happen without too much interference. Even very difficult emotions can move through the body in a healthy way, without the thinking mind judging them as negative. Blocking emotions, denying them, storytelling, victimizing—these are things all of us do to try to stay in control and stay safe. And yet if we recognize that we are creating our own thoughts, emotions, and experiences, we can realize that we get to create whatever we want in a different way. We can tell a different story. Don't worry if you don't know how to do that yet; just start small.

The psychologist and philosopher William James once said, "Our first act of freedom, if we are free, ought in all inward propriety to be to affirm that we are free."[49] So, what it is going to be? What do you choose? Freedom or safety? Will you run from fear, or run into it? The thinking mind concerns itself with keeping the body safe. Clear consciousness moves beyond bravery.

Rituals

The word *ritual* might have strong religious connotations for some, but my definition of it is more secular, less solemn. Think of rituals as special habits—a repeated, conscious set of behaviors that creates a meaningful experience. The thinking mind often views ritual as silly. But rituals open us up in ways the thinking mind cannot comprehend. As Blaise Pascal put it, "The heart has its reasons, which reason does not know. We feel it in a thousand things. . . . It is the heart which experiences God, and not the reason. This, then, is faith: God felt by the heart, not by the reason."[50]

By definition, a ritual calls on all aspects of the self. We can't sit alone in our room and perform a ritual in our head. In addition, rituals connect us to the physical world, very often incorporating one or more of the natural elements of earth, water, fire, and air. This is true of many of the most notable rituals still common in the modern world such as burial, cremation, and baptism. The aspect of time is also important in ritual, which often has a beginning, middle, and end. All rituals can lead us from one state, through an experience of some kind, and into a new state. (Think of a wedding, where partners arrive with one identity and leave with another.) We cannot "think" our way to this new place; we must experience it.

Just as with emotional practice, we can bring ritual into our lives in small, everyday ways. Here are a few ideas.

Exercise: Create a Personal Altar

You can build an altar in any quiet corner of your space, indoors or outdoors. It can be small and simple. Many altars start with a base of some kind—a small wooden table or a slab of rock could be a good choice. Pick colors, materials, and objects that hold meaning for you beyond your left-brain categorization of things. In fact, you may want to pay special attention to anything that the left-brain interpreter rejects as "too silly" or "wrong." These might be hints at something you're pushing away but would do better to integrate. You can incorporate fabrics, textures, images, trinkets, or symbols that have meaning for you. Candles, incense, or small bowls of water infused with herbs or scented oils can bring a sense of peace and healing. Your altar should feel welcoming—a place to ask questions of your deep inner knowing, a place to meditate, to come home to stillness and presence. Once you've practiced with your altar for a while, institute a regular cleansing ritual of the altar, refreshing all its elements to make sure it stays alive and vital.

Exercise: Make a Family Ritual

Lovely, nourishing rituals can be built around daily habits like mealtimes or going to bed. You could play "Thorns and Roses," a game where everyone shares something difficult (a thorn) and something wonderful (a rose) from their day. With little kids, a quick roughhouse or physical game of "the floor is lava" can sweat out some of the left brain's pent-up anxieties from the day.

You might also want to augment existing rituals around special times of the year or holidays. One family I know has a New Year's Eve ritual of writing down one or more things they would like to let go of from the previous year on one slip of paper, and on another one they write down one or more things they would like to invite into their lives in the upcoming year. These can be shared out loud or kept confidential. Then everyone tosses their slips of paper into a roaring fire, with good wishes. What are your holiday rituals? What might you do to expand them?

Exercise: Fallen Leaves Ritual

In many places in the world, this practice would be best to do at the beginning or end of fall, as trees are just beginning to shed their leaves, or as they are losing their last few.

Pick a single tree that has shed a good number of its leaves, perhaps in a grassy or gravel area where the leaves haven't covered every inch. Grab a bag and pick up all the leaves dropped by the tree. Then, sit at the base of the tree with your back resting against its trunk, and close your eyes if that feels comfortable. Feel the sensations of sitting on the ground, of the energy of the earth supporting you and the tree against your spine. Imagine that your body has energetic roots extending into the ground, and energetic branches reaching up into the air and sunlight.

When you're ready, open your eyes and pick up your bag. Your next task is to place the leaves again *as the tree would place them*. Consider how the tree would interact with its environment, and how the leaves would find their way to their most natural configuration on the ground. Feel your own roots and branches as you work, taking as long as you want.

This is an impossible task to accomplish with the left brain, whose narrow spotlight can never see the larger picture. The right brain perceives connections because it has a vast attention span. Think of watching a school of fish or a flock of birds; if you zoom out with the right brain, you see the whole, the interconnectedness, the dance. You can experience your body not as a separate thing from nature, but as part of the whole. There is no part where you end and it begins.

There is no correct way to do this exercise. Just try it. See what happens.

Exercise: Harnessing Randomness

We know that the left brain resists new information, doesn't like rethinking its categories and models, and hates branching out from what it thinks it knows. We also know that learning happens most effectively through novelty, play, and the ability to make mistakes. How can we integrate the two? One way to spark the learning capacity of the brain and enjoy yourself at the same time is to harness randomness.

If you are stuck on a problem, try using a random word generator online and commit to writing for three to five minutes about your problem, making connections to whatever word comes up. For example, imagine the word is *shift*. Set a timer and write about your problem, which, let's say, is that the baby is not sleeping through the night in the way they were last week. *Do we take more regular shifts and plan them in waking hours? What about shifting the location of the baby for a little while to see what happens? What about the idea that a baby's development from one stage to another—a kind of shift—also tends to come with regressions? Learning to walk means forgetting how to sleep for a little while. Maybe we can just honor the shift, and not freak out that this problem will last forever.*

The left brain will automatically make connections and start to spin out stories to link your word and your problem. The good news is that these will necessarily be new ideas, because you've likely never associated this word with this problem before. Push yourself to keep coming up with connections until your timer runs out, because your first ideas will often reflect your most basic conditioning. This can be a very powerful exercise in groups as well, with everyone throwing out ideas that the random word brings up for them.

Here are a few more simple ways to access randomness:

- Trying to decide between two low-stakes options? Flip a coin.

- Feeling anxious about how a new experience will play out? Pick three tarot cards or animal cards to spark imaginative connections for the beginning, middle, and end of the experience. (You don't have to believe in tarot or animal cards to get the neurological bonus of making novel connections.)

- Ask a friend to put three random "treats" in your calendar, such as "Go get an ice cream cone," "Take a long walk with the dog," and "Buy yourself a new notebook and pens."

Somatic Practices

Somatics is a way to approach bodywork, psychology, healing, and artistic practice through movement. The root *soma* in the word *somatics* refers to "the body as perceived from within." Rather than being concerned with the outside or performance qualities of movement, somatics centers on the internal experience and awareness of the body—on learning to decode what the body is saying. Many researchers say that the right brain is more embodied, because its representation of the body is far more extensive than that on the left side. Somatic practices help integrate both sides of the brain (with their respective strengths of spatial awareness and language/story) and ground them within bodily sensations. If we remember that the nervous system extends throughout the whole body, we can appreciate how this kind of practice might help us "lose our minds."

Some somatic practices include the following:

- Becoming aware of the breath, or practicing specific breathing patterns to achieve certain neurological results

- Mindful meditation

- Saunas and ice baths, which can support neurological and immunological function

- Somatic Experiencing, a body-based therapy for survivors of trauma and people with PTSD

- Many massage, strength, stretching, vocal, and posture modalities, including yoga, tai chi, qigong, the Alexander Technique, the Skinner Releasing Technique, the Feldenkrais Method, and Rolfing Structural Integration

We can incorporate somatic practices into anything else we're doing. Consider the somatic experience of driving, walking, arguing with someone, or learning something new. What is it like to do these things with an awareness from inside the body? Again, the left brain will consider this to be a useless idea, which means we're onto something.

Exercise: Box Breathing

If you think of breathing practices as too woo-woo or spiritual for you, I will offer that the following breathing technique is utilized by large numbers of first responders as well as active-duty military. It has been proven to help manage the stress response in the body in extreme circumstances, and it can help anyone who is experiencing anxiety or is in a situation that requires focus and calm. My students love this exercise because it is one of the easiest to remember and visualize.

In box breathing, you imagine making a four-sided shape with each of four breath activities: First, inhale a count of four; then hold the breath for a count of four; then extend your exhale over a count of four; and finally hold for a count of four before breathing in again. Repeat this cycle—in four, hold four, out four, hold four—for at least five breaths and for as long as you want. If it helps, you can use your finger to draw the square shape in front of you as you breathe. See how you feel, and if this changes your response in a high-stress situation.

Is Music God?

There is a wonderful documentary about the classical pianist and Holocaust survivor Alice Herz-Sommer, who lived to be one hundred and ten years old. She says two things in the film that strike me as important in her own life and applicable to many other lives: "Life is beautiful" and "Music is God."[51] Though we may not understand how she arrived at the insight that life is beautiful after experiencing so much suffering, we can understand the sentiment. The second statement is more confounding, though no less profound. How can music be God? What does this mean?

As a class project, I decided to do something without giving much instruction. Usually this annoys students, but this time it inspired them. I simply asked them to answer the question, "What does music mean to you?" I was blown away by the responses. From the viewpoint of the thinking mind, music doesn't really "do" anything for us outside of those few who have made careers from it. So why did it mean so much to every single student?

Music doesn't fill our bellies. It doesn't take away any of the dangers of the world. It can't be used to subjugate anyone, or to discover unknown facts or theorems. We don't get paid to listen to it, and only a small percentage of people get paid to create it. The thinking mind struggles to account for its value, yet music is essential to people and cultures worldwide. Here are some of my students' responses that might speak to the appeal, meaning, and value of music:

> "Music is something that I can feel in my soul. It's like having a bunch of best friends who are catering to you."

> "Everything that I felt as a child, whether it be the hot summer sun on a beautiful day, or how I felt riding with my father on the way home from a trip into town—listening to music explodes my mind with those exact same emotions from whatever memory I wish to go back to."

> "Music is in every aspect of my life. Everything from the way I dress to the things I believe is shaped by music."

Research confirms that listening to and making music are perhaps the only processes that activate almost every area of the brain. As we've discussed, the brain works in specialized modules, and any given task will typically light up only a select area. Music lights them all up. The emerging field of music therapy utilizes the whole-brain aspect of music to deal with the issues of the mind arising from memory loss, disease, or damage to the brain.

One reason music is so powerful is that it occupies the mind fully, distracting us from the thinking mind *without trying to*. When we listen to music, we are not trying to *not think*—we are simply not thinking. Furthermore, music is something we take in all at once, something the left-brain interpreter cannot do but the right-brain excels at. Music takes us beyond the thinking mind and taps into a more authentic version of who we are than we think.

Music's influence goes beyond the brain and into the rest of the nervous system and body. Research has shown that music can heal the brain and body. It can increase blood flow as well as lower heart rate and blood pressure. It can counter the effects of stress by reducing the stress hormone cortisol and increasing serotonin and endorphin levels in the blood. It's been shown to help manage and ease pain, and to strengthen endurance during workouts.[52]

We all came into this world with music, connecting to it long before we started overthinking everything. The human brain is hardwired to distinguish music, beats, and tones from other noise. Babies start to hum and dance and enjoy music long before they start talking. Many parents instinctively talk in a sing-song way to their newborns, and some (myself included) sang to their kids long before they were born. Research has shown that infants can recognize music they heard in the womb.

The philosopher Alan Watts once pointed out that "'You play the piano.' You do not work the piano."[53] There is a very different feel between work and play. Music is a form of play, and play includes curiosity, novelty, enjoyment, release, and learning. Music gives us a much-needed break from the thinking mind.

Many musicians have expressed that their best music often just "appears" in their minds; it's not something they think about, and they can't articulate the process. I particularly like the story of the song "For the Love of God" by guitarist Steve Vai. The melody came to him and he didn't know what to do with it, so he recorded it quickly and then put it away. Years later, he revisited it and turned it into his most popular song.[54] The rapper Jay-Z wrote in his autobiography that people think he makes up these great rhymes, but he says he doesn't—they just show up in his head.[55]

In this way, music "comes" to the thinking mind, rather than emerging from it.

To create means to bring into being. Creation is godlike. The mind would love to take credit for creation, and often comes up with a story that seems like a plausible explanation for a creative act. And it's true, the mind's clever tricks can certainly put us in the path of inspiration or open up our ability to receive creative impulses. In my view, music is the language of consciousness. Music is a dance that takes place outside of the mind's construct of time and its fiction of the self. In this way, it seems to me that Alice Herz-Sommer's view that "music is God" makes a lot of sense.

Practice: The Drum Circle

If you haven't been part of a drum circle, put it on your bucket list and make it happen. One common form of the drum circle is derived from ancient shamanic ritual or indigenous spiritual practices from around the globe. It also turns up in many other forms, such as Buddhist chants. At its most basic, a drum circle is exactly what it sounds like—people playing drums in a circle. It is remarkable how little instruction one needs for this, and I find it works best if you remind the thinking mind that it doesn't have to interfere. It will very likely get bored, anyway, and let the body and the right brain take over. When my class first did a drum circle exercise, we fell into it as if we had all done it many times before. The beat seemed to take on a life of its own. It lead us and we followed in collective rhythm.

To find drum circles in your area, try checking with your local music store, bookstore, library, or meetup.com.

Thoughts and Problems

If good happens, good; if bad happens, good.
—Lao Tzu, Tao Te Ching

By now you may be thinking, *All this no-self stuff is fine when it comes to philosophy, but how is it going to solve my problems?* Well, let's put it this way. Think about two very different experiences: the taste of French fries and the pain of a new burn on the skin. These may seem as different as different gets, and yet they are each the result of the nervous system processing body sensations. The same consciousness exists behind each. The "goodness" or the "badness" of either experience only exists in the judgment of the thinking mind.

The Buddha and neuroscience agree on this point. There is no difference between what we call desirable (the taste of French fries) and what causes suffering (a new burn on the skin). They are the same. From the Buddhist perspective, the problem only arises when the mind mistakes its experience for reality. Neuroscience confirms that we do not experience reality as it is, and the self that convinces us we do is only another fiction of the thinking mind. The only thing we know for sure is that we do not know.

Consciousness, it seems, busies itself with inventing reality. In other words, consciousness plays at being all the things in the world—*even those things you think are your problems*. We can tune ourselves to this fundamental reality, and can understand the dancing, shifting, timeless, formlessness that truly is, from the only access point we will ever have: the ever-renewing present moment. Modern science understands that we are stardust, and all matter is made up of energy. When we really understand this, our problems will literally resolve themselves, melting away like a star at dawn, or a flash of lightning in a summer storm. This process goes by many ancient spiritual names, including enlightenment, revelation, and insight. It is simple, but not easy.

When we mistake the form (our thoughts) for the formless (reality), we make the most common mistake the mind makes. Consciousness can take on an infinite number of forms. One of the most popular forms these days is thinking. While we've been thinking for thousands of years, one could say we've recently put thinking into overdrive. Some have thoughts they believe are about life, others have thoughts about what they think is the brain (we call this neuroscience). Some have thoughts they call spirituality. But there is simply no way to make the formless into a form. In other words, we cannot think about consciousness. We cannot think about who we truly are.

Yet just because we cannot think about something doesn't mean it isn't real. It doesn't mean that it is unimportant. It doesn't mean that it doesn't affect how we live our lives. It only means that we can't think about it. We are learning to use the mind rather than have it use us.

So how do we use the mind as a kind of portal to go beyond the mind? Some of the exercises that follow are meant to do just that. My general advice is to take things slowly, to design tiny experiments, to build up your intuition by grounding yourself in your bodily experience and your connection to the earth, to connect with others, and to cultivate a home in the realms of no self and no mind.

The Extra Horse

There is an old story about a man who left his three sons an inheritance of seventeen horses after his death. He left the eldest one half of his horses, the next oldest one third of his horses, and the youngest son one ninth of his horses. The thinking mind knows this is a problem because you can't divide seventeen horses in half, so you can't satisfy even the first son's inheritance.

A king offered the sons help in solving this problem by giving them an additional horse, making the total eighteen. Now the math worked. The first son received one half of eighteen, or nine horses; the second son received one third of eighteen, or six horses; and the third son received one ninth of eighteen, or two horses. When you add up the total of all the sons' horses, it comes to seventeen—the father's original gift. The king left with his additional horse.

In the solution to this "unsolvable" problem, the eighteenth horse was a placeholder, a symbol that helped satisfy the needs of the thinking mind. The same might be said of the role of thoughts for the thinking mind. Thoughts become placeholders that satisfy the thinking mind's need to solve problems. To me, the extra horse in this story is not unlike many theories of consciousness that rely on complex math and neuroscience: They make the problem seem solvable to the thinking mind.

This is where we are as far as the science of consciousness is concerned. Just as we are tempted to solve our mental suffering with more thinking, it's tempting to imagine that the thinking mind might solve what it sees as the problem of consciousness. The thinking mind wants consciousness to be a problem. It isn't. I hope that this book has shown you that consciousness isn't a mystery to be solved but an experience to be had.

Consciousness, quantum mechanics, gravity, and the meaning of our existence cannot be solved by thinking. Just because the mind thinks in categories doesn't mean that God does.

Take a glance at history and ask, When did thinking start? Did it start with the Big Bang, with the earliest forms of life? Regardless, whatever happened before thinking worked flawlessly without a single thought. Perhaps we are vehicles in which God thinks. We are the vehicles in which consciousness does all sorts of things. Those who have had a mystical experience have experienced consciousness beyond thinking. The universe has been not-thinking far longer than it has been thinking. It may very well go back to this state. A state of being aware of everything all at once.

The Dream of Thinking

Dreaming itself is strange and interesting. We know so little about this form of consciousness. (It may sound strange to think of dreams as conscious, but all major theories of consciousness consider dreaming to be a state of consciousness, not unconsciousness, like the other stages of sleep.) Even though we're convinced that our waking thoughts correlate with reality, when it comes to dreams, we accept that they break the link between consciousness and reality. Dreams are not real, but thoughts are? This should give us a clue about our thoughts, because the same brain that does the dreaming also does all the thinking.

I recently had a strange and interesting dream in which my two uncles were playing musical instruments that were not instruments at all. One had a large rectangle-shaped thing with strings and a mouthpiece like a bagpipe. It wasn't anything that made sense, yet in the dream that didn't seem to matter.

That's the point. In dreams, all sorts of things are what they are not: You are in a room, but it's not a room. You are with someone you know is your friend, but you've never seen this person's face in waking life. We know that dreams are not real, and within dreams we are prepared to accept all sorts of wild realities as though they are completely normal.

To wake up from the dream is to become aware of this paradox. Nothing in the dream is what it appears to be, but we only know this *after we wake up*. When we wake, we realize how strange it was to have believed the strange things that seemed normal during the dream.

Neuroscience still has no real clue as to why we dream. We do know that if we stop dreaming, all sorts of bad things happen to us both physically and mentally. Could dreaming have evolved for a deeper reason? Could dreaming remind us that the nature of this existence dominated by the thinking mind is also a dream? That is, a reminder that thinking pulls us into a dreamworld of thoughts? Perhaps we can integrate dreams into our clear consciousness.

In the East, many people understand that what we call a nighttime dream is simply a dream within a dream. The name Buddha means one who is awake. What would it mean to awaken from the dream we call ordinary reality? Taking thoughts seriously is one way in which this dream world pretends to be real. So perhaps taking these thoughts less seriously and putting a little distance between them and reality, as we've been doing in this book, is one way to start. We do this all the time in other contexts. When we watch a sad or scary movie, for example, we understand that this is a metaphorical experience; we are "playing" at reality, not having a real experience. What if we saw other "real" experiences as the playful metaphors they really are?

Consider the thinking mind's idea of how we got here: 13.7 billion years ago, the universe exploded from nothing; 3 billion years ago, life formed from lifeless matter and then eventually consciousness suddenly appeared. In the same way that something emerges from nothing in a dream, the thinking mind certainly seems to have followed a dreamlike path. This "dream" of the evolution of consciousness is the agreed-upon scientific version of the history of everything! A good reminder not to take anything too seriously.

One of the ways that the mind pulls us into the dream of thinking is by making us believe that thoughts are real and serious. The origins of the word *serious* are related to words like *heavy* and *weighty*. Thoughts that we take seriously weigh us down because we give them weight. Thoughts are actually harmless, but we suffer because we see them as literal reality. Then again, we also believe that the world is made of solid things, but physicists assure us the whole thing is just the potentials of energy. We believe things are what they appear to be.

The same thing happens in a dream. If we fall off a cliff in a dream we won't be physically harmed, but we may nonetheless scream and feel terrified. Most of our thoughts drag us down because we have mistaken them for actual reality.

Unreal things can cause very real suffering. And yet, if this existence is only a dream, why not enjoy it? If you've ever tried lucid dreaming you know how much fun it can be. Why not apply that same process to this dream we call reality? Wake up. Enjoy. If you want a sad dream or an adventurous dream with danger, that's okay too. Consciousness creates experience, and thinking is only one limited form of experience.

I hope that through trying the exercises and practices in this book you have already had some experiences of clear consciousness. Clear consciousness is who you truly are. It is the architect of this dream of reality. It is the dreamer of this dream and the creator of the mind. In this sense, while I have said over and over again that you are not the mind, in a sense you *are,* because you are the vastness of clear consciousness. You are the whole show—not just the one who dreams, but the one who invents the dreams and then decides to go to sleep on purpose.

You are already beyond the limited clouds that cast shadows of thinking in a dream world. The moment you realize that your mind isn't you, and that your self is a fiction, you can break free of the thinking mind. You, the real you, has always been outside looking in with clear consciousness. You are the architect. You are the director. You are the creator. And you are blissfully enjoying it all.

Practice: Waking Up to Lucid Living

There are some people who can wake while they are in a dream. Many spiritual teachers and ancient mystics cultivated this ability. Lucid dreaming means consciously staying in your dream. Scientific studies have validated that this kind of dreaming is authentic and distinct from other kinds of dreaming. That is, it isn't something that people made up or believe happened after waking.

There are many methods to help achieve this state. One way is called reality testing. You build this practice while you are awake, and then it will very often show up in your dreams. To begin, draw a *W* on the back of one hand and a *D* on the back of the other. Throughout the day, and whenever you notice the letters on your hands, ask yourself, *Am I awake (W) or in a dream (D)?* Answer briefly, out loud or internally, and then carry on with whatever you were doing. This becomes such a habit that you end up doing it in a dream, and presto! When you answer D in your dream, you have achieved a state of lucid dreaming, or awareness of your dream.

This exercise takes this practice up another level. On the back of one hand, make a *D* for "I'm lost in the dream of thinking." That is, *I'm thinking about reality rather than being in it.* On the other hand, make an *R* for "This is reality and not just thinking about it." As you go through the day, test over and over to see how much time you spend in reality. By recognizing how much of the day you spend lost in the dream of thinking, you can learn to wake up to the reality of clear consciousness.

Conclusion

The Mystery and the Metaphor

You have reached the end of this book, but I hope this is just the beginning of a lifelong practice of no self, and integration of clear consciousness. As I mentioned early on, in my own life, the convergence of neuroscience and Buddhist wisdom and practice has flowered into profound peace, understanding, joy, and ongoing curiosity. I enjoy working *with* my thinking mind as a tool, an instrument, a plaything. After all, the real you invented the mind. I would say it is the most thrilling act of creativity possible to hide something precious where we would be least likely look for it. As the old Hindu saying goes, "If God wished to hide, God would choose man to hide in. That is the last place man would look for God." The same goes, I think, for the real you, which is both hiding in plain sight and unseeable.

I want to extend an invitation to you. An invitation to play. To live life as a metaphor and a mystery, not taking it seriously but living sincerely.

What if we can integrate the thinking mind in a playful way, rather than trying to distance ourselves from it, destroy it, or deny it? By using this workbook, by actually *doing* the things that felt silly or useless, you have done exactly this. You first dissociated from your thinking mind and set down the heavy baggage of your illusory self. Then you learned to integrate the thinking mind into the clear consciousness that is you. This is the key to ending suffering.

It is said that the Buddha responded to his students' tales of their problems with laughter. You might find it surprising that people who joke about themselves have a higher overall well-being. As the Stoic philosopher Epictetus put it, "He who laughs at himself never runs out of things to laugh at." We suffer the most when we take our stories literally. The stories of work, money, and particularly the story of the self. The alternative is to understand our stories metaphorically, which can hold a deeper truth than so-called reality.

As an example, consider the world's religions. Humans have long endured fighting over which is the right or correct religion. But this conflict can only exist when each religion is taken seriously—that is, literally. All religions peacefully coexist when they are taken as metaphor.

What metaphors might we use to understand our existence, our precious life?

What if life is an escape room? This is a game where a group of people pay to be locked into a room, find clues, and solve puzzles in order to get out. Taken literally, this is ridiculous. Why pay to get locked in and struggle to get out, when you could just not go in the first place? But as a metaphor for life, it's quite revealing.

If clear consciousness is all knowing and all powerful, it lacks limitation. No surprises, no time ticking away, no challenges, no mystery. So maybe clear consciousness locks itself in a room of hidden clues and then goes on the adventure of finding its way out. Perhaps we enjoy escape rooms because they are a metaphor for the game we are playing, right now, called life. We fall asleep into the dream of thinking, because if we didn't there would be nothing to wake from.

Clear, infinite, unthinkable consciousness *created* the thinking mind so you could get totally lost in it and believe it was who you are. Perhaps you took the idea of the self very seriously, and you suffered. If these exercises were successful, perhaps you lost your mind and found your true self. It is a curious sensation when the clouds clear and you experience that the light of consciousness was there the whole time. You may even feel the urge to run down the street yelling, "I am consciousness!"

The thinking mind was never here to punish you, and the real you was there the whole time running the show. Have you ever looked all over for your phone and then discovered that it was in your hand or pocket the whole time? It's impossible not to laugh a little. To lose your mind and then realize it is all part of the game is a final artful act of integration.

You created the artwork called reality. You created limitation so you could be truly complete. You created the notion of being serious so that you could get lost, suffer, and experience the joy of coming home to a playful universe in the same way you laugh after looking everywhere for your phone, and then notice it was in your hand the whole time.

This is the bliss of no self, no problem.

Acknowledgments

Very few books happen in isolation, and I would like to thank the following people for wonderful conversations that helped improve the quality of this work: Deepak Chopra, Jill Bolte Taylor, Agah Bahari, Lara Patriquin, Jacob Nordby, Hale Dwoskin, Victoria Shaw, Sherry McAllister, Kevin Reese, Stuart Preston, Gary Lee Haskins, and Eric Zimmer. Deep thanks to my wife Janie and my kids, Zoe and Nick, for always embracing the strangeness this work brings to the family. Tremendous gratitude goes to Randy Davila and the insightful crew at Hierophant Publishing. In my more than twenty years of being a university professor, my students have taught me as much as I have taught them. I am grateful for their open minds and the risks they take in class to go off on adventures to new places and to boldly go where few have gone before. All of this comes together in this work. One cannot have a static, lifeless philosophy about the living, ever-changing process of reality and so I'm thankful for all the teachers that continue to come into my life.

Notes

1. Rumi, "We Can See the Truth in Your Eyes," in *Rumi: In the Arms of the Beloved,* trans. Jonathan Star (New York: Penguin, 1997), 3.

2. Alain Morin, "Self-Awareness Part 2: Neuroanatomy and Importance of Inner Speech," *Social and Personality Psychology Compass* 5, no. 12 (December 2011): 1004–1017.

3. Michael S. Gazzaniga and Joseph E. LeDoux, *The Integrated Mind* (New York: Plenum Press, 1978); Michael S. Gazzaniga, *Social Brain: Discovering the Networks of the Mind* (New York: Basic Books, 1987).

4. Michael S. Gazzaniga, *The Mind's Past* (Oakland, CA: University of California Press, 1998).

5. Michael S. Gazzaniga, *The Bisected Brain* (New York: Appleton-Century-Crofts, 1970).

6. Matthew A. Killingsworth and Daniel T. Gilbert, "A Wandering Mind Is an Unhappy Mind," *Science* 330 (November 2010): 932.

7. Andrea Zaccaro et al., "How Breath-Control Can Change Your Life: A Systematic Review on Psycho-Physiological Correlates of Slow Breathing," *Frontiers in Human Neuroscience* 12 (September 2018), https://doi.org/10.3389/fnhum.2018.00353.

8. Raymond S. Nickerson, "Confirmation Bias: A Ubiquitous Phenomenon in Many Guises," *Review of General Psychology* 2, no. 2 (June 1998): 175–220, https://doi.

org/10.1037/1089-2680.2.2.175; Peter C. Wason, "On the Failure to Eliminate Hypotheses in a Conceptual Task," *Quarterly Journal of Experimental Psychology* 12, no. 3 (1960): 129–140, https://doi.org/10.1080/17470216008416717. (While this study did not use the term "confirmation bias," it was the first to examine the concept using an example very similar to the one presented here.)

9. Peter C. Wason, "On the Failure to Eliminate Hypotheses in a Conceptual Task," *The Quarterly Journal of Experimental Psychology* 12, 129–140. Peter C. Wason, "Reasoning about a Rule," *Quarterly Journal of Experimental Psychology* 20, no. 3 (August 1968): 273–281, https://doi.org/10.1080/14640746808400161.

10. K. H. Grobman, (2003). Confirmation Bias: A class activity adapted from Wason's 2-4-6 Hypothesis Rule Discovery Task. Retrieved from: http://www.DevPsy.org/teaching/method/confirmation_bias.html.

11. R. C. Schank and R. Abelson, R. *Scripts, Plans, Goals, and Understanding.* (Hillsdale , NJ: Earlbaum Assoc., 1977).

12. Jerome H. Barkow, Leda Cosmides, and John Tooby, eds., *The Adapted Mind: Evolutionary Psychology and the Generation of Culture* (New York: Oxford University Press, 1995), 181–184.

13. J. Haidt, *The Righteous Mind.* (New York: Penguin Books, 2013).

14. This example is from the work of Hector J. Levesque, a Professor of Computer Science at the University of Toronto.

15. This and a similar example can be found in Robert L. Solso, M. Kimberly MacLin, and Otto H. MacLin, *Cognitive Psychology, 7th Edition* (Boston: Pearson, 2005), 426–434.

16. This example and others to follow are found with additional description in Keith E. Stanovich, *What Intelligence Tests Miss: The Psychology of Rational Thought* (New Haven, CT: Yale University Press, 2010).

17. Amos Tversky and Daniel Kahneman, "Evidential Impact of Base Rates," in *Judgment under Uncertainty: Heuristics and Biases*, ed. Daniel Kahneman, Paul Slovic, and Amos Tversky (Cambridge, UK: Cambridge University Press, 1982): 153–160.

18. Ralph M. Barnes et al., "The Effect of Ad Hominem Attacks on the Evaluation of Claims Promoted by Scientists," *PLOS ONE* 13, no. 1 (January 2018), https://doi.org/10.1371/journal. pone.0192025.

19. For those wanting to go deeper, here's a classic body scan from Jon Kabat-Zinn: https://www.youtube.com/watch?v=15q-N-_kkrU.

20. Betty Edwards, *Drawing on the Right Side of the Brain* (New York: Tarcher/Putnam, 1989).

21. "A Tried-and-True Method of Teaching Basic Drawing Skills," Official Website of Betty Edwards, accessed May 27, 2022, https://www.drawright.com/theory.

22. Iain McGilchrist, "Reciprocal Organization of the Cerebral Hemispheres," *Dialogues in Clinical Neuroscience* 12, no. 4 (2010): 503–515, https://doi.org/10.31887/DCNS.2010.12.4/imcgilchrist.

23. Pablo Andrés Contreras Kallens, Rick Dale, and Paul E. Smaldino, "Cultural Evolution of Categorization," *Cognitive Systems Research* 52 (December 2018): 765–774, https://doi.org/10.1016/j.cogsys.2018.08.026.

24. One of the first papers on the representativeness heuristic: Daniel Kahneman and Amos Tversky, "Subjective Probability: A Judgment of Representativeness," *Cognitive Psychology* 3, no. 3 (July 1972): 430–454, https://doi.org/10.1016/0010-0285(72)90016-3.

25. Robby Berman, "How Many Blue Dots Do You See?: The Science of Why We Overinflate Our Problems," *BIG THINK*, July 3, 2018, https://bigthink.com/mind-brain/one-fascinating-reason-things-never-seem-to-get-better/; David E. Levari et al., "Prevalence-Induced Concept Change in Human Judgment," *Science* 360, no. 6396 (June 2018): 1465–1467, doi: 10.1126/science.aap8731.

26. Andrew Huberman, "The Science of Gratitude & How to Build a Gratitude Practice," November 22, 2021, *Huberman Lab Podcast*, https://hubermanlab.com/the-science-of-gratitude-and-how-to-build-a-gratitude-practice/.

27. Larry R. Squire, "The Legacy of Patient H.M. for Neuroscience," *Neuron* 61, no. 1 (January 2019): 6–9, https://doi.org/10.1016/j.neuron.2008.12.023.

28. Brenda Milner, "Memory and the Medial Temporal Regions of the Brain," in *Biology of Memory*, ed. Karl H. Pribram and Donald E. Broadbent (New York: Academic Press, 1970), 37.

29. A. R. Luria, *The Mind of a Mnemonist: A Little Book about a Vast Memory*, trans. Lynn Solotaroff (Cambridge, MA: Harvard University Press, 1987).

30. Henry Roediger and Kathleen B. McDermott, "Creating False Memories: Remembering Words Not Presented in Lists," *Journal of Experimental Psychology Learning Memory and Cognition* 21, no. 4 (July 1995): 803–814. And the original study that came up

with the technique: James Deese, "On the Prediction of Occurrence of Particular Verbal Intrusions in Immediate Recall," *Journal of Experimental Psychology* 58, no. 1 (July 1959): 17–22, doi:10.1037/h0046671. Together this method is now known as the Deese–Roediger–McDermott paradigm.

31. William F. Brewer and James C. Treyens, "Role of Schemata in Memory for Places," *Cognitive Psychology* 13, no. 2 (April 1981): 207–230, https://doi.org/10.1016/0010-0285(81)90008-6.

32. "Summary of Cotton's Case," *Frontline*, PBS, accessed May 27, 2022, https://www.pbs.org/wgbh/pages/frontline/shows/dna/cotton/summary.html.

33. Todd Rose, "When U.S. Air Force Discovered the Flaw of Averages," *Toronto Star*, January 16, 2016, https://www.thestar.com/news/insight/2016/01/16/when-us-air-force-discovered-the-flaw-of-averages.html.

34. John Colapinto, "The Interpreter: Has a Remote Amazonian Tribe Upended Our Understanding of Language?" *The New Yorker*, April 9, 2007, https://www.newyorker.com/magazine/2007/04/16/the-interpreter-2.

35. F. Lhermitte, F. Chedru, and F. Chain, "A propos d'un cas d'agnosie visuelle [A Case of Visual Agnosia]," *Revue neurologique* 128 (1973); 301–322; S. M. Brambati et al., "The Anatomy of Category-Specific Object Naming in Neurodegenerative Diseases," *Journal of Cognitive Neuroscience* 18, no. 10 (2006): 1644–1653, http://www.ebire.org/aphasia/dronkers/the_anatomy_of.pdf; Lea K. Pilgrim, H.E. Moss, and Lorraine K. Tyler, "Semantic Processing of Living and Nonliving Concepts Across the Cerebral Hemispheres," *Brain and Language* 94, no. 1 (2005): 86–93; Mike J. Dixon, M. Piskopos, and T. A. Schweizer, "Musical Instrument Naming Impairments: The Crucial Exception to the Living/

Nonliving Dichotomy in Category-Specific Agnosia," *Brain and Cognition* 43, nos. 1–3 (June 2000): 158–164.

36. James L. Oschman, Gaétan Chevalier, and Richard Brown, "The Effects of Grounding (Earthing) on Inflammation, the Immune Response, Wound Healing, and Prevention and Treatment of Chronic Inflammatory and Autoimmune Diseases," *Journal of Inflammation Research* 8 (March 2015): 83–96, https://doi.org/10.2147/JIR.S69656.

37. *The Earthing Movie: The Remarkable Science of Grounding*, directed by Josh and Rebecca Tickell (2019), https://www.earthingmovie.com/.

For improving heart health: Howard K. Elkin and Angela Winter, "Grounding Patients with Hypertension Improves Blood Pressure: A Case History Series Study," *Alternative Therapies in Health and Medicine* 24, no. 6 (November 2018): 46–50; Glenn N. Levine et al., "Meditation and Cardiovascular Risk Reduction: A Scientific Statement from the American Heart Association," *Journal of the American Heart Association* 6, no. 10 (September 2017), https://doi.org/10.1161/JAHA.117.002218.

For brain health: Gaétan Chevalier et al., "Earthing: Health Implications of Reconnecting the Human Body to the Earth's Surface Electrons," *Journal of Environmental and Public Health* 2012 (2012): 291541, https://doi.org/10.1155/2012/291541; Ben Isbel et al., "Neural Changes in Early Visual Processing After 6 months of Mindfulness Training in Older Adults," *Scientific Reports* 10, no. 21163 (2020), https://doi.org/10.1038/s41598-020-78343-w.

For reducing anxiety: Gaétan Chevalier, Kazuhito Mori, and James L. Oschman, "The Effect of Earthing (Grounding) on Human Physiology," *European Biology and Bioelectromagnetics* 2, no. 1 (January 2006): 600–621; Maurice Ghaly and Dale Teplitz,

"The Biologic Effects of Grounding the Human Body During Sleep as Measured by Cortisol Levels and Subjective Reporting of Sleep, Pain, and Stress," *Journal of Alternative and Complementary Medicine* 10, no. 5 (October 2004): 767–776; Stefan G. Hofmann and Angelina F. Gómez, "Mindfulness-Based Interventions for Anxiety and Depression," *Psychiatric Clinics of North America* 40, no. 4 (December 2017): 739–749, https://doi.org/10.1016/j.psc.2017.08.008.

For well-being: Shian-Ling Keng, Moria J. Smoski, and Clive J. Robins, "Effects of Mindfulness on Psychological Health: A Review of Empirical Studies," *Clinical Psychology Review* 31, no. 6 (August 2011): 1041–1056, https://doi.org/10.1016/j.cpr.2011.04.006; Gaétan Chevalier et al., "The Effects of Grounding (Earthing) on Bodyworkers' Pain and Overall Quality of Life: A Randomized Controlled Trial," *Explore (NY)* 15, no. 3 (May–June 2019): 181–190.

38. Gaétan Chevalier et al., "Earthing: Health Implications of Reconnecting the Human Body to the Earth's Surface Electrons," *Journal of Environmental and Public Health* 2012 (January 2012): 291541, https://doi.org/10.1155/2012/291541; Gaétan Chevalier et al., "Earthing (Grounding) the Human Body Reduces Blood Viscosity—a Major Factor in Cardiovascular Disease," *Journal of Alternative and Complementary Medicine* 19, no. 2 (February 2013): 102–110.

39. Gaétan Chevalier, Kazuhito Mori, and James L. Oschman, "The Effect of Earthing (Grounding) on Human Physiology," *European Biology and Bioelectromagnetics* 2, no. 1 (January 2006): 600–621.

40. For a deeper description of motion, depth, and color processing in the brain, see E. Bruce Goldstein and James R. Brockmole,

Sensation & Perception, Tenth Edition (Boston: Cengage Learning, 2017).

41. For detailed descriptions of Kosslyn's work and experiments, see Stephen Michael Kosslyn, *Image and Mind* (Cambridge, MA: Harvard University Press, 1980).

42. Reverend Dr. Martin Luther King, Jr., *Strength to Love* (Boston: Beacon Press, 1981), 47.

43. Carl Jung, *Memories, Dreams, Reflections*, ed. Aniela Jaffé, trans. Richard and Clara Winston (New York: Vintage Books, 1989), 326.

44. Philip Brickman, Dan Coates, and Ronnie Janoff-Bulman, "Lottery Winners and Accident Victims: Is Happiness Relative?" *Journal of Personality and Social Psychology* 36, no. 8 (September 1978): 917–927, doi: 10.1037//0022-3514.36.8.917.

45. T. Wilson, et al. 2014, July 4. Just Think: The Challenges of the Disengaged Mind. *Science 345, 75. doi:10.1126/science.1250830.*

46. Oliver Sacks, *An Anthropologist on Mars: Seven Paradoxical Tales* (New York: Vintage, 1996).

47. Carl Jung, *Memories, Dreams, Reflections,* 247–248.

48. This is adapted from the work of Diana Chapman. Learn more at https://conscious.is/team/diana-chapman.

49. William James, *The Will to Believe: And Other Essays in Popular Philosophy* (New York: Longmans, Green, and Co., 1912).

50. Blaise Pascal, *Thoughts, Letters, and Minor Works*, trans. W. F. Trotter (New York: P. F. Collier & Son, 1910), 99.

51. *The Lady in Number 6: Music Saved My Life*, directed by Malcolm Clarke (2013).

52. Loomba, R. S., Arora, R., Shah, P. H., Chandrasekar, S., & Molnar, J. (2012). "Effects of music on systolic blood pressure, diastolic blood pressure, and heart rate: a meta-analysis," *Indian Heart Journal*, *64*(3), 309–313. https://doi.org/10.1016/S0019-4832(12)60094-7.

Mottahedian Tabrizi, E., Sahraei, H., Movahhedi Rad, S., Hajizadeh, E., & Lak, M. (2012). "The effect of music on the level of cortisol, blood glucose and physiological variables in patients undergoing spinal anesthesia," *EXCLI journal*, 11, 556–565.

Moraes, M. M., Rabelo, P., Pinto, V. A., Pires, W., Wanner, S. P., Szawka, R. E., & Soares, D. D. (2018). "Auditory stimulation by exposure to melodic music increases dopamine and serotonin activities in rat forebrain areas linked to reward and motor control," *Neuroscience Letters*, 673, 73–78. https://doi.org/10.1016/j.neulet.2018.02.058

53. Alan Watts, "Coincidence of Opposites," (Tao of Philosophy lecture series, April 16, 2019), https://alanwatts.org/1-1-4-coincidence-of-opposites/.

54. Joe Bosso, "How Steve Vai Wrote 'For the Love of God,'" *GuitarPlayer*, September 03, 2021, https://www.guitarplayer.com/players/how-steve-vai-wrote-for-the-love-of-god.

55. Jay-Z, *Decoded* (New York: Spiegel and Grau, 2011).

About the Author

Chris Niebauer earned his PhD in Cognitive Neuropsychology at the University of Toledo specializing in differences between the left and right sides of the human brain. He is a former professor of Slippery Rock University in Pennsylvania, where he taught courses on consciousness, mindfulness, left- and right-brained differences, and a course on artificial intelligence.

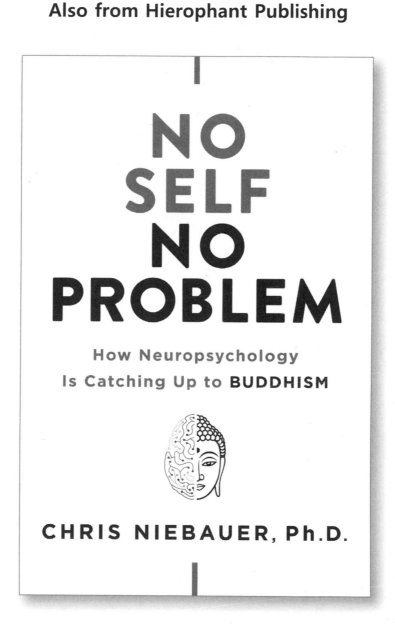

San Antonio, TX
www.hierophantpublishing.com